STRONGHOLD

THE SECRETS BEYOND THE WALL

BETH KINDER

Remade Ministries

Vacaville, California, USA

Published by Remade Ministries
Vacaville, CA 95687
www.remade-ministries.org

All Scripture quotations are from the New Living Translation
unless otherwise stated.

Edited by Laura Davis
Cover Design Katherine DiZio

Printed in the United States of America
ISBN-13: 978-1508663898
ISBN-10: 1508663890

Table of Contents

To

Tom, Kaitlyn, and Joshua

Thank You For Loving Me

When I Was Unlovable

Introduction

Throughout the pages of this book I open the doors into my life, because isolation and secrecy kill the soul, but conversation and community restore it. It's my hope that as I share my story it will give you permission to share yours.

While writing this book, I have envisioned the many places you might sit while holding it. I have imagined where you live, and the life you've led. I have wondered how the atmosphere mixed with these words might impact your heart. Every chapter began with a prayer. I always asked the Lord to go into the deep places of my heart so He might reach the deep places of yours. At times it felt like you and I had already met, as I would lean back in my chair and visualize the stories you would share if we sat down for coffee together.

It's not by accident you're reading this book. The Lord has pursued you, and He is anticipating His encounter with you. I want you to know He's always been there, seeking to catch your attention, desiring to reveal Himself to you, and longing for a deep relationship with you, the one He calls His beloved.

I believe that, if allowed, this book will take you to places you didn't even know you needed to go. God will touch areas in your heart where you were unaware you desired to be touched. The book will challenge the level of trust you give the Father, and the time you commit to Him. I guarantee you will come to a place where you'll tell the Lord you want more, and when you do He will be ready to give more to you.

You may need to read a chapter more than once. Don't be in a rush to get through the book. God delights in spending time with you, and He's already done the work—you just need to enter in.

The book is set up to encourage you to write your own story as you read the pages of mine. The Journal Your Journey is where you will record the stories and history of your life. We keep records of our bills, we list the daily responsibilities we must accomplish, but do we record the historic encounters we have with God? If you haven't begun journaling, I encourage you to begin through this book. I've never met someone who regretted recording their special moments with God. However, I have encountered countless who wish they had.

My journals helped me remember the raw moments shared here. They returned me to all the secret places where the Holy Spirit met with me. Your journal will record your raw moments, and one day you, too, will reread them as the victor, not the broken author.

—Beth Kinder

Acknowledgments

Many people helped get this book into print. My name may be on the cover, but without their help it wouldn't be in your hands.

First, I want to thank my husband, who has believed in and for me when I couldn't believe for myself. Tom, thank you for reminding me who I am when I couldn't see it. The prayers I heard you pray, and the ones I never knew about, are one of the only reasons I never gave up. Your covering carried me through. Countless moments are recorded in my journals where you have been the living, tangible presence of God in my life. Everything Love is, you've freely given to me, asking nothing in return. You are my best friend and my running partner with the Lord—He perfectly paired us so long ago.

To Kaitlyn and Joshua, thank you for enduring the stressful days recorded in the pages of this book. You are heroes in your own right. Both of you are incredibly strong and intelligent people who have challenged me to be a better version of me. Thank you for reminding me time and time again that I am a great mom, especially when I didn't act like one. You are my pride and joy. You are the perfect balance of the best parts of Dad and me. You have brought so much adventure to my life. You both are destined for great things, and I am so grateful I get to be a part of watching them unfold.

I could write another book when thanking the team at Remade Ministries. Kate DiZio, Sophia Rowe, Donna Hoover, and Stephanie Spencer are the champions behind the book. Their endless dedication to this project has humbled me. God knew what I needed when I didn't. It's been an honor serving the Lord with such a dream team. A special shout out goes to my East Coast sister Kate. Your generosity and humility are straight from the Lord Himself. Everyone on this project knows it would not have gotten where it needed to go without your incredible gifts and foresight. Although we all did our part, you made the magic happen. My gratitude for your friendship could never be fully expressed in this lifetime.

Just a few more thanks are needed before I close. My sweet Brandi Rennemeyer, our friendship was a divine connection. Thank you for sharing with me the reader's perspective; it dared me to be a better writer. Thank you Lisa Courtney for being my writing coach. You gave me the courage to begin. Thank you Laura and Jim Davis for ministering to those who have a story to tell and helping them tell it with excellence. To Pastor Mark Sligar, thank you for your wisdom and friendship to Tom and me, and to my church family, The Father's House. Your support for the call of God on my life is a treasured gift. You taught us to dream big because we serve a big God. To all of my prayer warriors, the ones known and unknown, you enabled it to happen because nothing is accomplished apart from prayer.

I have saved the best for last, so I really hope you made it this far. Until my life was laid out upon an altar, I wasn't really living. It was there I encountered You, the One who took my brokenness, breathed life into it, and remade it into what it was always designed to be. You gave me visions, dreams, and passions that were never there before. You challenged me to believe for the literal meaning of Ephesians 3:20. Thank You for taking the foolish one and writing her into Your story—I am nothing apart from Your grace. You made something beautiful out of the ashes of my broken life. I will live to bring You glory as long as I have breath. Again, I lay my stories upon Your altar for Your glory, because I know these stories are safest in Your hands.

Stronghold — The secrets beyond the wall

CHAPTER 1

The Stronghold

The Lord is good, a stronghold when trouble comes.
He is close to those who trust in him
Nah. 1:7 (ESV)

The Counterfeit Stronghold

Lord. Help. Me. The distraught cries from a desperate place where apart from God, there is no hope. It's not the type of prayer we hear at a church meeting or in a small group. This prayer we scream out while pounding our fists on a tear-soaked floor hidden behind the bedroom door. In the horribly messy moments of life, that is the prayer I have found myself praying—simple but direct.

Abraham Lincoln said, "I have been driven many times upon my knees by the overwhelming conviction that I had nowhere else to go. My own wisdom and that of all about me seemed insufficient for that day." Motherhood has left me time and time again feeling insufficient for the day, but motherhood marked by a hormonal disorder has driven me to my knees on more than one occasion with the conviction there was nowhere else to run.

During my second pregnancy I began having severe bouts of depression and intense feelings of rage. I had never felt rage like I was experiencing while pregnant with our son. I thought it was the vast amounts of testosterone floating in my system. I would even joke about it. Little did I know my entire body makeup was changing while carrying that little boy in my belly.

In moments of distress my prayers rarely contained biblical scriptures or fancy Christian dialogue. Instead, they were the simple cries of a desperate woman, broken and in need of a rescuer, but too afraid to let Him all the way in. During those times, I needed God more than I needed any other. Yet, in the early years God was not the first on my rescue list; too much shame littered the road marked to Him. I put my husband, friends, and close family on the throne that was meant only for my Savior. Yet, even with them I was never totally honest, because I didn't really want them to know the truth anymore than I wanted God to be involved.

Those I loved seemed to have it all together. I looked at their lives and saw only perfect worlds all wrapped up in the Christian life. Their children obeyed, marriages seemed so godly, and relationships with the Lord seemed worlds away from mine. All I had to do was take one glance at my private life and know I could never measure up. So I let them in just enough, without exposing the real me. If I let them in too much they would know what

I knew—that I was just a fake. Sharing with them was completely controllable. God, on the other hand, was absolutely unpredictable. I didn't know what to expect if I allowed Him in. Fire and brimstone just didn't seem appealing.

The years prior to my diagnosis I had two little ones only two years apart in age, and a husband deployed 9 months out of 12. There were times I literally thought I was going out of my mind. I cannot tell you how many times I wondered if I had a Dr. Jekyll and Mr. Hyde curse. For a few weeks I could handle just about any crisis life could throw at me. I was a military wife after all. I felt stable—normal even. No sudden outbursts, no insane thoughts, no major meltdowns. I was in total control. Then for no apparent reason, all of that would change. Something my husband would say, the kids too loud, or the stress of the bills would set it off. Once I was wound up not much could bring me down until there was an explosion.

It wasn't until my little guy was about four years old that I was diagnosed with Premenstrual Dysphoric Disorder, otherwise known as PMDD. I call it PMS on steroids. It's all of our typical PMS symptoms magnified to some unmanageable degree. They say a person can be either suicidal or homicidal—I don't ever remember wanting to hurt myself, so I will leave it up to your interpretation where my mental pendulum swung.

After the rage bubble would burst, I'd look behind me at the shattered mess of a stunned husband and crying children. I would stand there ashamed of my actions and distraught over the woman I had allowed to come out. Visions of my girlfriends and women I knew would flood my mind in condemnation. Their perfect lives would haunt me. I couldn't stand the woman I was, and I didn't dare let those with perfect lives into my less than perfect life. I couldn't reach out to my friends; these moments were just too shameful to share with another.

The isolation of nowhere to go was almost worse than the episodes of rage. The solitude of my thoughts left me alone to have extensive conversations in my mind, using words I wouldn't speak over my worst enemy. I believe it was the isolation that brought me to my knees. Yet, being on my knees left me empty. God was not healing me, and I was not changing.

I was tired of finding myself time after time saying the same line of repentance for the same outbursts of rage. I wanted to find permanent freedom from this insane life I was living. Not just for myself, but also for those I loved the most. In my eyes, I was destroying the people I would otherwise die for. But, would God deliver a crazy woman?

The Pursuit for More

I wanted my relationship with God to grow to a place where I could live out Psalm 118:8, "It is better to take refuge in the Lord than to trust in people." I needed God to move from being my last call for help to my first line of defense if I was ever to find freedom from this nightmare.

My hunger for God to deliver me from this insanity thrust me into his Word and daily prayer like never before. I hadn't yet been diagnosed, so I thought that if I stayed in that place long enough, if I believed big enough, I would be set free from this rage and anger. Little did I know the journey would unearth more than being set free from my cycle of insanity. My pursuit uncovered a relationship that healed places I didn't even know were begging to be set free. As I started to pray for a solution, the Lord revealed time and again my lack of trust in Him. Over and over He showed me that I didn't know Him as well as I knew my spouse, my friends and my family. As a result, I trusted in their counsel more than God's.

I pursued a deeper knowledge and a closer relationship with the Lord. I asked for one that would be stronger than any personal relationship I had on earth. Looking back, I see I asked in ignorance. I was unaware my pursuit would test what little faith I possessed, reveal how weak my trust was in Him, and expose how shallow my understanding was of a relationship with the Trinity (God the Father, God the Son, and God the Holy Spirit). Unsuspectingly, God began to lavish upon me the most unfathomable, untainted, and purest form of undeserving love I'd ever experienced. He patiently drew me into His presence, as I danced in and out of this relationship commitment. The Holy Spirit would touch a place I didn't want to go, and I would run away only to find myself back at His feet asking Him to heal where He touched. It was our own dance, and He was the best partner.

During those dance lessons, He showed me who He wanted to be in my life. He wanted to take me and hide me, heal me, strengthen me, and change me from the inside out. Psalm 18:1–2 says, "He is my fortress, my safe place, my refuge and my stronghold." God became my STRONGHOLD. Nothing and no one could reach me as long as I was abiding in the presence of the greatest fortress ever known. I had no need, I had no shame, and I only knew hope when I was there. Friend, this is the place I want to take you, and this is the journey we will go on together.

The stronghold was my lifeline as I navigated the waters of PMDD. When I got my diagnosis I thought there would be a resolution to my nightmare. I was sadly mistaken. As the doctors tried to find a medication that would manage my disorder, God sifted through years of childhood memories, spiritual attacks, and biblical confusion. There was no quick fix to my prayer, "Lord, help me."

The years of my journey were laced with so much confusion outside of the stronghold. However, the more I immersed myself in scripture, the more order, patience, and protection I found myself in. His stronghold was now my safe zone.

I learned that when abiding in the stronghold of the

Lord, whether I am at my worst or soaring at my best, His position with me remains the same and His protection never waivers. I also learned that in times of trouble God is kind, patient, and very near regardless of what I am personally feeling at the moment. The most beautiful revelation of all was that I don't have to hide in His protection only during the storms of life. He calls me to hide in Him, in His stronghold, *every day* of my life. Are you ready to go there?

The Authentic Stronghold

Webster's definition of a stronghold is, "a place that has been fortified so to protect it against attack." The Thesaurus uses synonyms like "castle, fortress, refuge, security, cave, tower, and defense".

In the Old Testament, a stronghold was a literal place. When Israel's enemy, the Midianites, invaded their land, the Israelites found refuge in strongholds (Judg. 6:2). God sent David and his 600 men to the stronghold in the wilderness to escape the pursuit of Saul (1 Sam. 23:13–14). Everything David needed for survival was found in the stronghold. The prophets spoke of a stronghold as a place of peace and safety in the Lord.

> The Lord Almighty is with us; the God of Jacob is our stronghold. (Ps. 46:11)

The Word says that while David was hidden in the stronghold, even though his enemy sought him, God did not allow Saul to find him. In the stronghold set by the Lord, the outside enemy could not penetrate through God's protection. His people were sheltered until it was safe to emerge. Friends, just rest on that thought for a moment. When we are hidden in the stronghold of the Lord and our enemy is in pursuit of us, God's stronghold shields us. It's our own personal cloaking device. Now, tell me you wouldn't be up for that type of superpower!

For everything good that comes from the Lord, the enemy places an evil counterfeit to ensnare God's people. There is a stark contrast between the fifty or more Old Testament references of a stronghold to the one New Testament stronghold referenced by the Apostle Paul. Where the Old Testament stronghold was a literal place to keep the enemy out, the New Testament stronghold keeps the enemy in. It's a fortress designed by our adversary to keep us captive in a stronghold of our mind.

> We are human, but we don't wage war as humans do. We use God's mighty weapons, to knock down the strongholds of human reasoning and to destroy false arguments. We destroy every proud obstacle that keeps people from knowing God. We capture their rebellious thoughts and teach them to obey Christ. (2 Cor. 10:3–5 NLT)

The Apostle Paul uses the analogy of a stronghold to describe a resistance to knowing God—a stronghold of human reasoning, false arguments, and proud obstacles. Can you imagine that stronghold my friend? Everything

Paul describes in 2 Corinthians 10:3–5 comes from our internal thoughts. Can you see the walls of our mental castle laced in human reasoning, and a spirit of intellect where individuals have no need for God? The towers of our minds thick with proud obstacles, which are fortified with anything that sets itself high above God, such as success, money, careers, families, ministries, or relationships. The mental gates are built with false arguments found in world religions and cults that teach of an earned path to heaven, or many roads which lead to the same god. The stronghold of the mind will demand an allegiance of our affection and dedication. These fortresses encapsulate the mind and build a barrier that prevents us from ever finding the authentic refuge of the Living God.

Wage War

The counterfeit stronghold has the power to destroy a believer's walk by means of deception. Paul makes it clear that this is a fortress we must wage a spiritual war against, not a physical one.

> For a time is coming when people will no longer listen to sound and wholesome teaching. They will follow their own desires and will look for teachers who will tell them whatever their itching ears want to hear. They will reject the truth and chase after myths. (2 Tim. 4:3–4)

Centuries ago when one kingdom wanted to overthrow another the armies would weaken the walls of the stronghold and then advance to take the city. Today, dear friend, the Kingdom of Heaven has come to take down the kingdom of darkness in our mind. This begins when we enter into His stronghold and allow Him to tear down the emotional and mental walls we've built around us.

The counterfeit stronghold has one single purpose: to prevent those of us who are free in Christ from living out our freedom abundantly. Every believer was liberated from captivity at the cross, but we don't always know how to live in the freedom we've been given. Through this book, you will learn to fight your enemy as the Israelites learned to fight theirs—through the power of God.

Joshua chapter 6 describes the taking down of a stronghold. The Israelites were facing a river that stood between them and the land God promised them. God parted the water, and His people crossed on dry land. They moved into their promised land only to face their first stronghold—Jericho.

> But the Lord said to Joshua, "I have given you Jericho, its king, and all its strong warriors. You and your fighting men should march around the town once a day for six days. Seven priests will walk ahead of the Ark, each carrying a ram's horn. On the seventh day you are to march around the town seven times, with the priests blowing the horns. When you hear the priests give one long blast on the rams' horns, have all the people shout as loud as they can. Then the walls of the town will collapse, and the people can charge straight into the town." . . . When the people

heard the sound of the rams' horns, they shouted as loud as they could. Suddenly, the walls of Jericho collapsed, and the Israelites charged straight into the town and captured it. (Josh. 6:2–5; 20)

The Israelites did their part, and obeyed the Word of the Lord, and God did what they could not do—He tore down those walls. My friend, we will wage a war against our enemy just as the Israelites waged a war against theirs. In obedience to God's Word, we will fight with His power and His weapons, and He will do what we cannot do in our own strength—tear down our walls.

God's plan for the authentic stronghold is that we would be so sure in Him, so grounded in Him, so confident in Him, so close to Him that we would live in the ultimate life-sustaining power of the Holy Spirit. He wants us to utilize the authority that we have been given through the power of the cross, to resist the lies of the enemy and not be taken captive by sin. He will show us a way around every temptation. He will open our eyes to the deception of the enemy, and He will do the very thing we cannot do for ourselves—set the captive free.

Tools for the Journey

Throughout this book we will touch upon key things that open our eyes to the counterfeit stronghold and equip us to enter into the authentic. Our responses to them will determine our success. You will find obedience to the word of God, knowing the character of God, and abiding in His presence are weapons for war and tools for overcoming.

Within the journey you will be tempted to quit. The enemy will confuse you, and there will be some things you may not even want to deal with. Just remember, it's in His stronghold we are healed, restored, and released into freedom. God's heart for us is to become so fused with Him that we are no longer easily ensnared or drawn to the stronghold of the enemy.

Throughout my journey, I found myself weaving in and out of human reasoning and obstacles of pride. However, it was the lies of false arguments that sent me on a quest to be set free from the insanity I found myself in. I had no idea how many of these false arguments stemmed from my childhood and past events. They were lies that told me I had to be good enough, perfect enough, strong enough, holy enough, and that no matter what, I needed to make sure I was enough for God. Otherwise, He would just pass me by for someone better.

As you take this journey with me, God will map out your road by revealing your captivity, showing you a way out, teaching you how to stay out, and open your eyes to pitfalls that will draw you right back into captivity. Then you will discover the absolute victory that comes from abiding in the presence of God.

In each chapter you will be encouraged to sit before the Lord with questions and instructed to wait for His answers. I encourage you not to rush this part of the study, as God will make an exchange during this time.

> And I will give you a new heart, and I will put a new spirit in you. I will take out your stony, stubborn heart and give you a tender, responsive heart. (Ezek. 36:26)

The Lord will soften your heart, making it pliable and impressionable. Here He will imprint scriptures, visions, and lessons custom made for you.

Let's begin by inviting Him into your quiet time right now before we go further.

> *Father, we know you see our hearts in all their frailty, faults, goodness, and strength. Help guide us today as we seek to find the truth of where we've strayed from you and believed in false teachings. Show us where we've relied on our own will power, determination, and self-help to guide our walk to freedom, instead of knowing you, drawing from your wisdom, your forgiveness, and your love. Reveal to us the counterfeit strongholds in our lives.*
>
> *In Jesus' name we pray, amen.*

Testimony of Truth
My Story:

> *For years I battled the fear of being exposed. My worry didn't come from a deliberate sin I was hiding. I was afraid that once people got past the surface level of my life, and knew the real me, they'd see the mess of numerous imperfections and decide to move on. If I could control what they saw, then I could control the outcome of the relationship. The more I stepped out in ministry, the more the Lord began prompting me to share my story of His healing. I was so guarded around others and so confused about why God would want to expose me. I couldn't see the liberty He was trying to bring to me.*

> *One day the Lord prompted me to share a very intimate part of my life with my Bible study girls. I was terrified and convinced that once I told them the truth they would all leave my group. As I prepared for the meeting I came across a Psalm.*

No one who trusts in you shall ever be put to shame. (Ps. 25:3)

> *Every time I began to panic over the thought of letting them into my hidden places, I would quote that scripture. I have continued to this day using Psalms 25:3 as a weapon to tear down any argument of comparison or doubt that wants to*

resurface. It has allowed me to let the world into my life.

Renee Swope said, "We were created to live in the light in such a way that our life stories tell about the light and our confidence in Christ draws others to the light."[1]

—*A Confident Heart*

The enemy's plan was to keep me hidden in the shame of my past so that I would not be able to live my future in freedom. He didn't just want to keep me from living out my freedom; he wanted to keep others from living theirs. God's plan is never to shame or expose us. It's to set us free so that we can help others be free, too.

> He comforts us in all our troubles so that we can comfort others. When they are troubled, we will be able to give them the same comfort God has given us. (2 Cor. 1:4)

God's stronghold brings a confidence to allow others into our lives and to boldly share our story with another. Throughout this study God will ask you to be brave and share with the women in your group or a trusted friend. Your obedience will be the conduit between God and another sister's "ah-ha" moment. Your courage will set others free because you started the conversation that everyone else was afraid to begin.

Journal Your Journey

- Take time to ask the Lord what the counterfeit strongholds are in your life. Write in your journal the first words that come to your mind. You may have more than one counterfeit stronghold.

- Look up in the dictionary the definition of the words you've written down.

- Write down any revelations their definitions bring to you.

The Battle Is the Lord's

The journey to discovering and knowing God is found through scripture, and getting there will be a battle. The enemy isn't one to give up real estate he has taken possession of. Nevertheless, like Jericho, your battle is the Lord's fight.

> The Lord will fight for you; you only need to remain calm. (Exod. 14:14)

As we prepare for battle, God will establish whose responsibility is whose on the frontline. God's job is to fight and His people's job is to remain calm. When staring at our war zone of captivity, the enemy is loud and intentionally intimidating. So, of course God would have to command us to do what is not naturally natural. No one remains calm in a battle, especially women! Our adrenalin rises about as quickly as our voices. Yet, the Lord commands us to remain calm in the face of our accuser.

Journal Your Journey

- Write Exodus 14:14 in the journal.

- Write in the journal any revelations from the Lord.

Our response in battle determines our success. Maybe you're a panic Paula, or neurotic Nala. Maybe you believe the worst in people. Or maybe you're a shameful Sheila and quit after you stumble. God wants to show you a new way of doing battle, and it begins with remaining calm and looking to Him. Before you pick up your phone and text your friend, call your husband, blog your woes, or tell your tales on Facebook, make sure you've first been before the Lord. It's time to tune our ears to the Father and bend our knees to the ground.

When the armies terrified King Jehoshaphat and all of Judah the Lord said, "Do not be afraid or discouraged because of this vast army. For the battle is not yours, but God's" (2 Chron. 20:15).

Today, my friend, the Lord says, *the battle is not yours but Mine. You don't have to listen to the taunting of the accuser, because I have given you authority and weapons to overcome him.*

Journal Your Journey

- Write out what your default response is during a battle.

- Write out why you feel it is difficult to remain calm in battle.

- Next to your default responses write how God would call you to respond.

- Look up Ephesians 6:13–17. Write out verse 17 and underline the weapons listed in that verse.

Our Stronghold Foundation

God has given you His salvation and His Word as two foundational weapons. The original battle was fought and won for us at the cross, and victory became ours at salvation. The everyday battles are now waged for our authority and influence. These are won through the power of the Holy Spirit as He reveals truth through His Word. Before I can take you any further in this study, we must address these foundational weapons and ensure you possess them both.

Maybe you don't know Jesus personally, or maybe you knew of Him once and have forgotten when you last sat down with Him and had a conversation. Perhaps you are not assured of your salvation, or you feel the Holy Spirit prompting you to get your life right with God. You will know that God wants you to say this prayer because your heart is racing and you have felt a longing to know more of Him throughout this entire chapter. If that's you, take a moment and say this prayer:

> *Father God, I know my life is a mess right now. I know that I'm not right with you. I know that I need you now more than ever before. I pray that you will forgive me of my sins, restore my life, and bring me into a right relationship with you. I pray father God that from this day forward you will show me the truth of your Word, how it applies to my life, and help me to come to know you more.*
>
> *In Jesus' name I pray, amen.*

Romans 10:9 says, "If you confess with your mouth that Jesus is Lord and believe in your heart that God raised him from the dead, you will be saved."

The path to knowing God will always be through knowing Jesus. Jesus tells us in John 14:6, "I am the way, the truth, and the life. No one can come to the Father except through me." The road to knowing Jesus will always be through the word of God. "In the beginning was the Word, and the Word was with God, and the Word was God" (John 1:1).

Over the course of this study your journals will become filled with incredible insight into the character of God, understanding of His Word, and a revelation of the Holy Spirit. You will record praises to the one who rescues you from the stronghold of the enemy. In the Psalms, King David often wrote of God's protective stronghold and the faithfulness of God. David would sing praises to God describing their personal relationship. You will find that your journal becomes your very own personal psalm book.

> *Father God, I have such a desperate need for you in every part of my daily life. I see my need for your Word in my life. I declare today by faith, in spite of what I feel, that you are my strength, my rock, my fortress, my deliverer, my God, my shield, my salvation, and my stronghold. I believe that every day I pursue you more; you will reveal the truth of each one of these attributes of you in my life.*
>
> *In Jesus' mighty name I pray, amen.*

If you made things right with God today and prayed the prayer of salvation, I encourage you to share this with a friend, pastor, or group leader. You can even email me at beth@remade-ministries.org. If you do not attend a life-giving church, or you do not know how to find a local church, please contact me and I would be happy to help you find one.

CHAPTER 2

A Friend For the Journey

It is not by force or by strength, but by my Spirit,
says the Lord of Heaven's Armies.
Zechariah 4:6

There was a woman who went walking down a road, and through her travels on that road she found herself in a horrid pit. She had heard about pits like this, but the road seemed laced with pleasure, power, and control. She believed she would avoid the pitfalls of the road and be able to enjoy the pleasures without the pain. Nevertheless, like the many before her, she too found herself at the bottom of a dark and ugly place.

The bottom of that hole was laced with shame, isolation, condemnation, and overwhelming hopelessness. It attached itself to her like thick black tar. Each time she would find her footing to get out of the pit, she'd slip and end up swimming in the sludge of shame that filled the dark place. When she finally made her way out, she swore, "I will never do that again."

It didn't take long after the woman was out that she found herself thinking about that road and all the pleasures she encountered. She began to justify her need to take a walk down that alluring road again. With the same intentions as last time, she determined to avoid that pit. But as if that miry place had a mind of its own, she found herself right back in the sludge of darkness. Frustrated and ashamed, she retraced the painful steps of failure back out again, asking herself, "Why can't I just stay away?"

The woman looked at her friends who no longer traveled that road of empty pleasures. They had overcome the pull of that dark ditch, and their lives were full and happy. She wanted what they had. The road that once looked so pleasurable had taken her farther than she had ever dreamed it would take her. It stole more from her than she had ever wanted to give. She whispered, "If I just try harder, if I just start over again, I know I can beat this. I know I can be who I want to be."

One day, the woman came upon someone who she felt knew her, saw her, and had a strange way of drawing out of her the pain of the past. Free from judgment and condemnation, she felt a trust she'd never known fill her naturally suspicious heart. No one had ever seen her like this person did. No one had ever trusted her like this person trusted her. One brisk morning, the two of them came upon the road she had battled for so long. The draw of that road and the memories of her past had all faded. The past had been replaced by a hope of her future with Him. Her liberation came when she trusted her Companion, Jesus Christ, who showed her that the past had no power over her future. He had wiped the slate clean.

The Need For Him

Charles Spurgeon said, "The first link between my soul and Christ is not my goodness but my badness, not my merit but my misery, not my riches but my need."[1]

We live in a world that promotes self-help and the self-made man, and it defines weakness as second-class. Yet, our first connection with God comes through our inabilities not our abilities. Once He saves us it doesn't mean we know how to walk in freedom. The not knowing can cause us to lean on human reasoning, and the enemy will guide us back down the self-help, self-made road and leave us believing our greatest connection to God is what we can do for Him, and not what He wants to do through us. We will end up living in a stronghold of proud obstacles where we believe it is our goodness that keeps us connected and useful to God.

The Israelites were physically delivered from slavery, but they walked in the desert for 40 years because their minds remained in bondage. They were a free people living in a slave mentality. They saw God as a deliverer but they didn't intimately know Him as Friend.

The Battle of Sin

The reality is that our battle with sinful temptations, addictions, and lust do not go away because we become saved. In fact, they actually become an even larger magnet, because now we know what we should not do, and the draw to do what we should not do becomes even more powerful.

The very purpose for the Law of Moses was to make known the inability of mankind to save themselves, and reveal the need for a Savior. The law itself aroused the desires of our heart and flesh and caused them to surface, revealing man's powerlessness over sin. As Believers in Christ, we are no longer under the Mosaic Law, but we can be saved, and still live under a law-like mentality.

A law-like mentality places restrictions to control the outer part of a person's actions through self-denial in an attempt to stay holy and right with God. It freezes the believer at the salvation encounter, but hinders them from developing a relationship with Christ. Then, when the Christian attempts to stay in right standing with God on their own, and fails, the condemnation leaves no hope for restoration. A person with a law-like mentality will usually turn, run, and hide from God because they only feel condemnation and not conviction.

Sin, Not a New Believer Problem

In the church, we tend to label sin as a new-believer issue. We are expected to know how to "avoid" sin the longer we serve God. The struggle to do what is right is not a new-believer issue, it's an every-believer issue. For those of us who have been saved awhile, we may have tackled what some would consider the "bigger sin" issues earlier in our walk. We may even have a tendency to think, "I'm good." Ignoring sinful pride, consuming idolatry, or incessant rage because it doesn't seem nearly as drastic as having an affair, watching pornography, sleeping with our boyfriend, or a drug addiction. It's a dangerous path to travel when we grade our sins on a curve. Sin is sin, and while God chooses to address our sin as He sees fit, Paul warned us not to think we're above falling into sin.

The Apostle Paul, at approximately 60 years old, and having been a mature Christian for twenty to twenty-five years, wrote, "I don't really understand myself, for I want to do what is right, but I don't do it. Instead, I do what I hate" (Rom. 7:15).

Paul was far from a new believer when he wrote that. He was at the height of his ministry. He fervently prayed for hours in a day, he worked miracles, and wrote numerous letters to the churches. He spoke before governments, kings, and rulers. He was a mature believer, and his life was completely Christ-centered, yet he stilled struggled with sin.

Martin Luther, the man who wrote the *Ninety-Five Theses* and unleashed the saved by grace doctrine upon the Church, struggled with his own sinful nature and inability to please God. He is known for saying, *Simul Justus et Peccator*, which means simultaneous saint and sinner.[2] The battle with his own weaknesses and his longing to please God led to the reformation of the church, and a deeper understanding of God's free gift of grace. One would think that with an understanding of God's grace, he would be free from the struggles of sin. However, historians describe Martin Luther as tormented by doubt, depression, and the fear of never being able to lead a holy enough life.

In Weakness

An enemy is most powerful if they can get a spy on the inside and destroy an army from the inside out. Our enemy, Satan, has come to destroy us from the inside out! He can create an overwhelming feeling of powerlessness if we allow sin to take an unchecked role in our lives. Nevertheless, sin, evil, and all our struggles point to one thing, our need for a mighty, gracious, and all-powerful God to overshadow sin's demand on our lives.

Maybe like Paul, Martin Luther, Spurgeon or even the woman in the story, you too are also aware of your weaknesses. Maybe you've thought, *I've tried this before; I cannot go down this road and end up disappointed again.*

26

Like us, the Apostle Paul longed to do what was right but knew that finding anything good in himself was impossible. Paul said, "And I know that nothing good lives in me, that is, in my sinful nature. I want to do what is right, but I can't. I want to do what is good, but I don't. I don't want to do what is wrong, but I do it anyway" (Rom. 7:18). Paul saw that in light of God's holiness, his best was still pathetic and his worst utter wretchedness.

I will never forget the day I realized it was my constant perseverance that kept the gaze and attention of God. He was not impressed by my most spiritual day, and He was not turned off by my worst Christian day. He was pleased with me just because I kept standing back up and showing up. Up until that revelation, I found myself in an ugly cycle like Martin Luther, never feeling like I could ever get it right.

Sister, can you see you're in good company when you're disappointed in yet another one of your failed attempts at doing what is good?

Journal Your Journey

- List some of the roads you keep returning to.

- Be honest before God and write about your fear of failing.

In Romans chapters 6–8, Paul addresses the very real struggle of sin. He writes about our natural tendencies to try to overcome sin by living a good life, (our law-like mentality) and the failure it brings apart from the saving grace of Jesus Christ and the power of the Holy Spirit. Paul makes it clear over and over again that, because of our salvation in Jesus Christ, we are no longer subject to, slaves of, captives of, or bound in sin and death. He repeatedly states we've been given a new life in Christ, one that should be lived as a new person. Our freedom comes when we daily live in the grace Christ showed us, not as believers but as sinners.

God's grace invades us when we allow Him to touch the places we want to keep hidden—just as He did with me in Chapter One. The power to look at those places free from shame and guilt will not come in your own strength, but through the strength of the stronghold. Wherever you carve out time in your day to be with God and in His Word, I encourage you to spend time in Romans chapters 6–8. Our understanding of this power, and the ability to find the truth in the word of God, is a pillar of the authentic stronghold of God. Don't underestimate the value of looking up these particular scriptures in this chapter.

Journal Your Journey

- Let's pause and look up in our Bible Romans 6:6–7.

- Read the scripture and write down what it means to you in your journal.

- In light of these verses, journal your thoughts about the road you described earlier.

Not a Slave

Apart from Christ, we would obey our old ways even if we didn't want to. Paul said that we were slaves to our sin (Rom. 6:20).

What does it mean to be a slave? A slave is to be bound in servitude as the property of a person or household, one who is subservient to a specified person or influence. I can attest to feeling like I was bound to rage for years. Have you ever felt like a slave to your sin?

When rage was my response to life's stresses, I felt like I served that ruthless master. I would cry out to God begging for deliverance, but my lack of trust in Him kept my mind in bondage long after my body was free from the rage. My slave law-like mentality would send me back into bondage each and every time, because of the unrealistic expectations I set up for myself. The good news is, as believers we are no longer a slave to our old life; we've been set free through the work of the cross. In 1 Corinthians 6:19–20, Paul says we now have a life of freedom, full of the power to do things that lead to holiness and to live a life that results in eternal life with God. That scripture shatters the law-like mentality of do good to be good, and shows us that there is a power in us that leads to holiness.

Today, even though your spirit lives in 1 Corinthians 6:19–20, your mind might look at past attempts and attempt to prove to your heart you're still a slave to sin. You may even want to toss this book across the room and quit the study because of the condemnation you feel from it.

Conviction -vs- Condemnation

Here's the problem: we are deceived when we are stuck in the counterfeit stronghold. Believing that we personally hold the power to set ourselves free is one of the 2 Corinthian 10 strongholds—a powerful deception that keeps us from knowing God. The very thought that we hold the ability to set ourselves free goes against the truth of God's Word. It's a mindset that shields us from any need of God in our lives.

Each time we fail to free ourselves, the enemy torments us with a blast of condemnation for yet another failure. The condemnation creates a divide between Christ and us, blurring the lines of conviction and condemnation. We become captives to our failures, and freedom seems just beyond our reach.

The condemnation breeds shame. Shame causes us to want to run and hide from God. We see another failed attempt, we recognize the disappointment in the eyes of those we love, we feel the disappointment in ourselves, and it doesn't take any stretch of the imagination to believe God must be disappointed with us too. It can feel like a familiar path around the same mountain.

Conviction is different from condemnation. Where condemnation causes us to want to run from God, conviction draws us to God. When God convicts us of our sin, it brings a full revelation that we are totally ill equipped to free ourselves from this battle. God's conviction always highlights our need for Him. His conviction will always produce a desire in us to want to do better, and a longing to be closer to Him. The beauty of our God is that His convictions do not come out of yelling, harsh punishment, or rejection as the world would impose. His conviction comes in that moment when He loves on us, even though we deserve anything other than love. In that moment we draw closer to Him to know more, and knowing Him more becomes the power that leads us to holiness. Then we leave the false stronghold of the enemy and find rest in the authentic stronghold of the Lord.

Testimony of Truth
Kim's Story:

> *Kim was raised in a church pew from birth. She loved the Lord and dreamed of being in ministry. She had been serving since she was a very young child. Yet, she was in bondage. She was wrapped*

up in a spirit of lust, bound in pornography. She wanted to be free, but she was powerless to set herself free. Kim found herself connecting with strangers on the Internet, sexting and sending revealing photographs of herself.

Kim's secret kept her hidden in sin and shame. She would attend church throughout the week, repent at the altar, only to find herself back in the web of lust by Friday. The bondage engulfed her life, causing her to eventually give everything away to someone who could have cared less.

Discarded by the man, her sin began to eat at her. She loathed herself and felt condemned by God and by those who knew. Anticipating God's rejection, as so many men before had rejected her, she ran as far away from the church as she could.

Away from the only life she knew, Kim bent a knee before the Lord and confessed. God's response was not the condemnation she had anticipated, but one of love. In that moment when Kim deserved love the least, she received it extravagantly.

It was the unconditional love of Jesus, and His acceptance of her, that shattered the walls around Kim's heart. In a moment His conviction drew her to repentance, and her repentance opened the floodgates to His love. His love became her stronghold in the moment when she was weakest.

Kim felt as though she should be judged, but she found mercy. God's mercy inspired her to want more of Him. Kim could now see how her sin had desensitized her heart to the conviction of the Holy Spirit. And the condemnation she heard wasn't the voice of God at all, but the voice of the very enemy who tempted her in the first place. His lies are what drove her into hiding from God.

She began to ask the Lord to help her overcome her temptations, and show her a way out of them. As Kim listened to the conviction of the Holy Spirit and immediately obeyed His convictions, sin lost its grip. The release of captivity from sin increased the power of the Holy Spirit inside her.

Journal Your Journey

- Keeping in mind the difference between conviction and condemnation, write out which one you've been listening to and record your insights.

- Ask the Lord to reveal His truth to you.

Our Need for All Three

The only way to live a full and powerful life as a believer

is to develop an intimate relationship with the Godhead. We will never live an overcomer's life with a superficial relationship with God, treating salvation like fire insurance, or completely ignoring the presence of the Holy Spirit. We must pursue a balanced relationship with God the Father, God the Son, and God the Holy Spirit, because each plays an important role in our victorious life.

In Exodus 17:8–16 there is a physical battle which perfectly depicts our need to have The Father, The Son, and The Holy Spirit actively involved in every detail of our lives.

In the battle of Rephidim, Joshua led Israel's army in a war with the Amalekites. Moses stood on the hill with his arms stretched out holding his staff. As long as Moses' arms held his staff in the air, the army would remain victorious, but if Moses lowered His staff, they would fall to defeat. So Aaron and Hur stood by the side of Moses and held up his arms, and the army defeated the Amalekites.

The Amalekites are descendants of Esau, and he forfeited his inheritance for a bowl of soup because he was hungry. In this fight, the Amalekites represent our battle with sin, and our willingness to give up God's best for our lives for an immediate gratification.

As Moses stood in a posture of surrender, he held the staff up high. His staff represented the authority of God. Moses could not hold up His authority alone, so Hur stood on the left side of Moses and Aaron on the right.

Hur means "liberty" and Aaron means "teacher". The Bible says, where the spirit of the Lord is there is liberty, and in John 13:13, Jesus confirms His name is teacher. Here in the battle, Hur represents the Holy Spirit on Moses' left; Aaron represents Jesus on his right.

As believers we are in this very same war with the Amalekites. To defeat our own sinful desires we must go into battle with a rod, an Aaron and a Hur. We must enter every battle with God's authority, the power of the Holy Spirit, and the wisdom of Jesus Christ. When we battle the flesh, we must take a posture of surrender, which covers us with God's authority, and leaves room for us to be flanked on either side by the power of the Holy Spirit and the wisdom of Jesus Christ, positioning us for the same victory Israel received.

The Holy Spirit brings liberty, otherwise known as freedom, to the battle. Jesus brings redemption, the way to restore all things as they were intended to be. God reigns above us, solidifying our identity and confirming to whom we belong. It's a beautiful picture of the authentic stronghold we've been gifted to take refuge in.

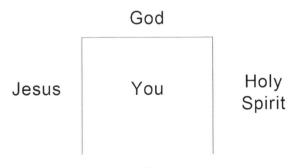

After the battle with the Amalekites, Moses and the Lord made a declaration. Moses built an altar and declared the Lord was his Banner, then said, "They have raised their fist against the Lord's throne, so now the Lord will be at war with Amalek generation after generation" (Exod. 17:16). A banner is a declaration of who an army belongs to and whose name they fight under. Moses declared that day, Israel belonged to the Lord, and it was by His name they would fight. In response the Lord declared that for generations to come, He would do their fighting.

As believers, we stand under the same banner as Moses, and we behold the same promise from God. When the war of the flesh rises to fight against the spirit of God that lives in us, it is not our power that will fight the enemy of the flesh, but the power of the Holy Spirit.

Our Power in Battle

As we take refuge in the authentic stronghold, we encounter a secret weapon given to every believer. That weapon is known as the Holy Spirit, and he teaches us a new way of living (Rom. 7:6).

Some of us have been in church a long time. We understand how to "do church" but we never learned how to live by the Spirit, because we've never been properly introduced to the Spirit, and His purpose in our life.

In order for Jesus to reach the whole world He knew He would have to die, because remaining on earth He was limited to time and space just like the limitations put on any other human. Jesus' death would bring to us another.

> And I will ask the Father, and he will give you another Advocate, who will never leave you. He is the Holy Spirit, who leads into all truth. The world cannot receive him, because it isn't looking for him and doesn't recognize him. But you know him, because he lives with you now and later will be in you. (John 14:16–17)

In this scripture Jesus shows the oneness of the Triune God, all three persons functioning in their unique but separate roles on our behalf. By asking God, Jesus recognizes God as the authority, and He [Jesus] positions Himself as the gateway to God. Then He introduces Himself as the Holy Spirit, and the Holy Spirit as His replacement when He leaves.

When Jesus introduces the Spirit, He also describes His character by choosing to call Him "Advocate". In the Greek it is *allos*, meaning "another of the same kind; comforter, helper, intercessor, and counselor." The word comes from the word *paraklétos*, which literally means "close beside, to make a call, to testify."

Jesus was assuring His disciples things were changing for the better. He explained God who was once known only through the pages of their Torah, had now made Himself known in the flesh, and was not leaving them behind. He now would be residing inside each one of them. Pause on that my friend. God went from being a distant God, to a personal God, and now an intimate God within them. Oh, the comfort in knowing God is not satisfied with anything less than an intimate relationship with us, and that intimacy with God is directly connected to our relationship with the Holy Spirit.

> I tell you the truth; anyone who believes in me will do the same works I have done, and even greater works, because I am going to be with the Father. You can ask for anything in my name, and I will do it, so that the Son can bring glory to the Father. (John 14:12–13)

The more intimate our relationship is with the Holy Spirit, the greater our power becomes. The power of the Holy Spirit is the same power that parted the Red Sea, defeated enemy nations, opened blind eyes, and endured the suffering of the cross. That power now resides inside the frail bodies of you and me, just waiting for the permission to mightily move through us.

Journal Your Journey

- Write what type of relationship you feel you have with the Holy Spirit—unknown, distant, personal.

- Write a prayer telling Him the type of relationship you desire to have with Him.

- Ask Him for a strategy to help you develop it.

The Promise in the Power

The presence of God in us produces the power of God through us. How we respond to the Holy Spirit in us will determine how He responds through us. Romans 8:31 says, " . . . if God is for us then no one can be against us." Understanding the same power that parted the Red Sea resides within us brings greater understanding that our enemies really do not possess enough power to ever defeat us.

If you've been attempting to live your Christian life without acknowledging the person of the Holy Spirit, then you are living a less than powerful life, and you're vulnerable to deception. Jesus said that the Holy Spirit will lead you into all truth. If we are living a life aside from the power of the Holy Spirit, we are living a life in our own strength. Living in own strength leaves room for the enemy to condemn us with our own actions and mistakes.

Paul reminds us:

> So now there is no condemnation for those who belong to Christ Jesus. And because you belong to him, *the power of the life-giving Spirit has freed you* from the power of sin that leads to death. (Rom. 8:1, *emphasis mine*)

The promise of freedom is directly linked with the Holy Spirit. Our ability to access that freedom comes through our relationship with the Holy Spirit. When we start each day with the mindset of *I will start over today and I will do better*, then we start our day in our power. However, if we acknowledge His presence in our life and our need for His power, then we begin each day with Him. Only then can we live a life outside of condemnation, and have an ear intently tuned to the voice of Holy Spirit, enabling us to quickly yield to conviction.

The Protection of Conviction

Our obedience to the Holy Spirit's conviction is the ammunition that destroys the enemy's lies and enables us to live a life of freedom and grace.

> Sin is no longer your master, for you no longer live under the requirement of the law. Instead, you live under the freedom of God's grace. (Rom. 6:14)

Apart from the power of the Holy Spirit, it is impossible to see the truth.

> When the Spirit of Truth comes, he will guide you into all truth. He will not speak on his own but will tell you what he has heard. He will tell you about the future. (John 16:13)

Truth convicts as a form of protection. It warns us of things in the future we cannot anticipate in our present circumstances.

Journal Your Journey

- In your Bible look up and read Romans 8:31–39, answering the following questions:

- Who can be against us? (Rom. 8:31)

- Did God spare anything for us? (Rom. 8:32)

- Will God give everything to us? (Rom. 8:32

- Why can't charges be brought against us? (Rom. 8:33-34)

- What are we called? (Rom. 8:37)

- Can anything ever separate us from Christ's love? (Rom. 8:39)

Be patient with yourself during the journey of this study. There is no quick fix, only a daily surrender if you are desperate for His covering. Remember, Adam and Eve walked with God. Moses carried God's tangible glory upon His face, and heard the audible voice of God. The disciples walked with God in human flesh, and yet all of these people stumbled. How much greater faith does it take for those of us who have neither seen nor heard God's voice, yet we still believe? Life is hard, we stumble, we stand back up and we stumble again. These are the very things that cause God's grace to abound all the more. Our stumbles do not activate His grace, but our will to stay the course does.

Father God, the closer we draw to you the more desperate we become for your presence and your power. We know apart from you we can do nothing and through you we have the power to do all things. You are our victory and our great reward. Father, we praise you that you left nothing to chance and made a way for our victory here on earth by giving us the companion of the Holy Spirit. We see that you have not left us to this on our own, but you've given us the victory through Him. Today we will begin a new walk by honoring Him, abiding in Him, talking with Him, leaning on Him, and surrendering all to Him day in and day out. Thank you, Holy Spirit, for who you are in our lives, for your wisdom, peace, truth, and comfort. We ask for more of you to come through our everyday lives.

In Jesus' name, Amen.

CHAPTER 3

He Loves Me, He Loves Me Not

We know how much God loves us and we put our trust in His love. God is love, and all who live in love live in God, and God lives in them.
1 John 4:16

He loves me . . . he loves me not . . . he loves me . . . he loves me not . . . Doesn't that bring images of an emerald field, a spring breeze, and a young girl lying on her back pulling one white daisy petal after the other? Do you remember being that girl? Counting ahead to see if you had enough petals to ensure he loved you, and if you landed on "he loves me not" you'd ditch the flower for a new one. I know I did!

Conditional Love

For years that was how I determined whether I was worth loving. My successes determined that I could be loved, and my failures forfeited love. Everything in my life was based on conditions, especially my relationship with God.

One of my earliest memories of conditional love is when I returned home from Youth Camp where I had recently dedicated my life to Jesus. My attitude and focus was completely different. My new attitude caught the attention of my dad, and he seemed so proud of me. I felt like he really enjoyed being around me. However, that lasted about as long as my newly dedicated life to Christ. As a teen, it didn't take long for the world to become more interesting than going to church. Friends and partying held my attention longer than Sunday school and church choir practice. I remember the farther I drifted from God, the worse my relationship with my dad became.

As an adult, I rededicated my life to the Lord. However, I carried that conditional love as an adult. I would base my Christian duties, such as reading my Bible, praying, or serving at church, to the depth of how I perceived God's love for me. I can remember getting ready to teach and running through a must-do list out of fear that God would not show up.

Everything I did had a value attached to it. If I was a good Christian girl it was like depositing credits into a bank that I could withdraw for love. Yet, if I messed up, not only could I not withdraw from my love account, I also subtracted any good I had already done.

I was a master at a life of conditional love imposed upon a God who loves unconditionally. For some of us, years of rejection have made unconditional love seem like a fairytale. So being able to accept that type of love from God doesn't seem possible. Some of us have been hurt so deeply by those we love, it's difficult for us to see God as a loving God.

Journal Your Journey

- Take a moment to write down how you view the character of God.

- Do you think of a loving God when you think of God?

- What type of person do you think God would love?

Deceived by Love

Through media and our culture, love has been watered down to hearts, flowers, couples, and romance. For so many, love has been simplified as a feeling, or sex, and when they don't exist neither does love.

Journal Your Journey

- Describe in your own words what you think love is.

Rebecca's Story

He was so handsome! I couldn't understand how someone like Donald could love someone like me. He was older than me, and he knew so much about everything. I had never been in love before. I surrendered my whole heart to this handsome and wickedly romantic man!

Almost immediately he talked about love, our future, and marriage. I thought I had found my Prince Charming. I was so taken by how romantic and attentive he was about everything. He showered me with serenades and love notes. His attention to detail and remembering everything we talked about made me love him more. He loved what I loved, and we had similar dreams.

He liked to pick out my clothes, and always asked where and who I was with. I just thought he was being protective and that he wanted to be a part of my life. My parents were the first to notice something strange, but I refused to listen. Then my girlfriends raised red flags, and so I distanced myself from them.

It seemed like the first month was the best, and after that I think I just stayed in hopes the man I first met would return. He never did. His concern turned to control. His questions turned to accusations, and every time he was mad it was because I was never enough. Where I once felt like I was living a dream, I was now living a nightmare. His love was conditional to how good I could be, and to him I was never good enough.

A painful past can barricade our heart to any possibility of ever letting love in, even God's love. These barricades can keep us from the safety of God's stronghold. Our inability to open up and trust obstructs our ability to know the very character of God. It's a Catch–22. The love that can heal us from brokenness is the love we are protecting ourselves from.

Very few of us, because of our own brokenness, can fully understand that there is love so deep and so real that it empowers us, enables Christ to make a home in our hearts, keeps us strong, and brings fullness and power to our lives. However, the apostle Paul describes such a love in Ephesians 3:16–19. He said that all God's people should understand it, yet not just understand it—experience it, and not just experience it, but be made complete through it.

Our lives are comprised of a variety of love encounters, both good and bad. A loving memory from a grandparent or friend, mixed with a painful memory from a lover or family member, all make up our perspective and expectation of love. They dictate how we receive love and how we express it.

When trust is broken walls begin to form around the heart where love once resided. Insecurities and suspicions push out trust and confidence. Knowingly or unknowingly our physical relationships influence our supernatural relationship with God. We begin to believe that how we love or have been loved by others is how the Lord responds to us in love. It completely influences how we respond and develop an intimate relationship with Him.

Like No Other Love

In this chapter I want to break the mindset that God's love compares to any human love we've ever experienced before, whether that experience was positive or negative. By the end of this chapter I want you to know the difference between God's love and human love. I want to empower you with knowledge of God's character when it comes to love, so you will be as convinced as the Apostle Paul was when he wrote Romans 8:38.

> And I am convinced that nothing can ever separate us from God's love. Neither death nor life, neither angels nor demons, neither our fears for today nor our worries about tomorrow—not even the powers of hell can separate us from God's love.

For if you can be as certain as the Apostle Paul was, then no matter what you face in the future, regardless of your successes or your failures, you will be assured of one thing forever—God's love for you is never based on what you can do; it's based on who He is. When you understand that, you'll never fear rejection again. Not from people and not from God.

Worth Loving

Most of us love through an if/then filter. For example, Rebecca felt that if she were the type of woman Donald wanted, then he would love her. When I was younger, I believed that if I was a good Christian girl, then God would love me. What we are actually seeking isn't love, but approval.

We equate approval to love and disapproval to rejection. When we filter love this way approval equals acceptance, and acceptance means, "I love you because you are worth loving—you've earned it." The painful opposite of this is that disapproval now equals rejection and rejection means, "I don't love you, because you are not worth loving."

Not worth loving… isn't that our greatest fear? That there is something inside of us that cannot be loved and therefore we will end up alone. It's the ultimate rejection to be unlovable. So we reject people before they have the opportunity to reject us, simply because we are afraid they will see we aren't worth it. Or, we pretend to be someone we are not, always changing the way we look and act just to be accepted in order to feel worthy of love. Secretly, we fear they will find out what we already know, that we're not worth the effort.

The question remains: Can we believe we are worthy enough for real, healthy, godly love?

The love we allow ourselves to receive is a direct reflection of the answer to that question, because we will accept the love we feel we're worthy of. When we cannot look inside ourselves and find a reason to love what we see, then we will only accept a love equal to our own self worth.

Friend, who told you that you weren't worth it? Who left a mark on your heart that now filters every relationship through a spirit of unworthiness?

Journal Your Journey

- Take a moment to list those who have marked your heart and spoken over your life that you were not worth it.

- Write out who they were and what they did, then go down that list one by one and say: "I am worth loving. I forgive you."

- Dear friend, don't wrestle with forgiving them. Your forgiveness is not saying what they did was right. Your forgiveness is unlocking your prison door.

My Story:

My biological father doesn't know I exist. My stepfather raised me from the time I was six months old. Around the age of eight, my cousin innocently let the secret out in the backseat of the car. My poor mom, unsure how I would respond, sought counseling on the best steps forward. My stepfather said he would adopt me, but years and years passed and it never happened. At sixteen my parents divorced, and in the legal papers my dad denied I was his child. In my eyes he was my father, but in his eyes I wasn't his daughter. Those words of denial branded me as—unworthy. I wasn't worth adopting, and I wasn't worth being called his daughter. For years I lived my life trying to prove my worth to him and everyone on that side of the family. I wanted to be one of them; I wanted to be loved by them. Nothing I did made me feel worthy enough on the inside to be accepted on the outside.

Over the years while raising our children, building a ministry, and even writing this book, I've heard that same whisper—*not worthy.*

Want to know something—*it's not a lie*. I'm definitely not worthy; but I wasn't chosen because I was worthy, I was chosen because I was willing!

My worthiness doesn't come from my willingness; my worthiness comes from the empty tomb. A tomb that was emptied before I was even born, and was emptied because God saw me worth it. Jesus fought death and won for me, *personally*. He fought Satan knowing I would sin, walk away from Him, and ultimately deny Him. The Lord went into battle understanding that even after I would believe in His name I'd mess up again and again. Nevertheless, he still found me worthy of the fight, and He finds you worthy of it too.

Jesus fought for me when I wasn't worth fighting for. No one had ever loved me in that way before. His battle for me marked me worthy, and that mark overrides any mark of unworthiness my birth had placed upon me.

My dear friend, that revelation of my worth didn't come from the mouth of a preacher or a book I read. It came from the secret place. It came from resting in His stronghold. It's the most powerful place you can be. It is in this place He reveals things that will alter the course of your life, as they have altered the course of mine. These revelations change mindsets you've carried your whole life. Don't forsake this journey! Keep pushing through. The Lord has revelations for you just like He had for me.

Today, when the enemy comes and whispers that I'm unworthy, I don't even pay any attention to it, because I am well aware I am not. But Jesus, whose spirit lives inside of me, is more than worthy. And He's chosen me not because of my worth to man, but because of my worth to Him. Because He said I am worth it, I am willing to say yes to whatever He asks—qualified or not.

My worth does not dictate His love, but His love proves my worth. He loves me because He is love. It's not the type of love that's conditioned through the if/then filter. It's a love that exists only because God exists.

He Is the Noun, We Are the Verb

"For God is love" (1 John 4:8). Friend, there is a vast difference between human love and God's supernatural love. These scriptures give a clear picture of God's love for us, and the biblical description of love.

- See how very much our Father **loves** us, for he calls us his children, and that is what we are. (1 John 3:1)

- Dear children, let's not merely say that we *love* each other; let us show the truth by our actions. (1 John 3:18)

- Dear friends, let us continue to *love* one another, for **love** comes from God. (1 John 4:7)

- Anyone who does not love does not know God. For God is **love**. (1 John 4:8)

53

- God showed how much he **loved** us by sending his one and only Son into the world so that we might have eternal life through him. (1 John 4:9)

- This is real **love**—not that we *loved* God but that he **loved** us and sent his Son as a sacrifice to take away our sins. (1 John 4:10)

- No one has ever seen God. But if we *love* each other, God lives in us, and his **love** is brought to full expression in us. (1 John 4:12)

- We know how much God **loves** us, and we have put our trust in his **love**. God is **love** and all who live in **love** live in God and God lives in them. (1 John 4:16)

- As we live in God our **love** grows more and more perfect. (1 John 4:17)

- Such **love** has no fear, because perfect **love** expels all fear. If we are afraid, it is for fear of punishment, and this shows that we have not fully experienced perfect **love**. (1 John 4:18)

The Bible describes two types of love in the above scriptures. When love is used as a noun I have highlighted it in bold. When love is used as a verb I have italicized it.

The love that is a noun in the Greek is called: *Agapé*: n. an *active* love. The word "active" means "to produce".

In the scripture 1 John 4:8 "God is Love," the word "love" is *agape*. This type of love would only cease if God ceased. The love that is a noun cannot change what it is, cannot stop what it is, cannot refuse what it is, and cannot withhold what it is.

The love that is a verb in the Greek is called: *Agapaō*: v. *to* love. The word "to" indicates *movement* towards a person, place, or thing.

In the scripture John 13:34 "…love one another," the word "love" is *agapaō*. This type of love means we are to give to another, and because it's a verb it can be started and then stopped at any time.

1 John 4:8 says that God is love, and Job 10:11 says that man is flesh and bones. The synonyms for the word "is" are "consists, comprised, contains".

If we were to re-write those scriptures using the synonyms it would look like this:

God consists of love.
God is comprised of love.
God contains love.

Man consists of flesh and bones.
Man is comprised of flesh and bones.
Man contains flesh and bones.

Do you see it? God can no more stop loving you than you are capable of living without your flesh and bones. Love is who God *is*! It is what He is made up of. Friend, we are the verb, and He is the noun. Because we are the verb, we filter and condition love, but because He is the noun, He cannot condition who He is. God can no more stop loving you than you can stop being a human. This is why God's love is incomparable to any love we've ever received before.

Who God literally *is*, we give *to* others. We choose whom to love and whom not to love. We can start and stop at any time—God cannot. He does not and cannot start and stop at will. It is impossible. This is why God's love for us is never conditional, and never based upon how good or bad we are.

> And may you have the power to understand, as all God's people should, how wide, how long, how high, and how deep his love is. May you experience the love of Christ, though it is too great to understand fully. Then you will be made complete with all the fullness of life and power that comes from God. (Eph. 3:18–19)

Understanding that Love is God and God is Love, you have the power to visualize the width, height, length, and depth of His love. For the very width, height, length, and depth of God himself is the measure of His love. The book of Job says, "Can you fathom the mysteries of God? Can you probe the limits of the almighty?" We can now see why Paul says it's too great to fully understand. For as infinite as our God is, He is equally infinite in His love. There is freedom in knowing the measure of God's love for us literally has no end to it.

Return now to the page that lists the scriptures in First

John. Over every italicized love place a V for verb and over every bold love, I want you to place N for noun. Re-read them with your new understanding of which love is your kind, and which love is God's.

Unconditional Love

Before today, it may have been easier for us to make God's love a verb, equating His love to approval, and comparing it to what we've experienced in past relationships. Now that we understand God's love for us is based completely on who He is, and has nothing to do with who we are, it breaks the lie that His love equals approval and smashes any measuring rod of worthiness. When the lie is broken, we can remain confident in the limitless Love of God and more aware of the limiting love of others. God's love is the purest, safest, and most reliable love. When the world fails around us, God never does.

We learned in 2 Corinthians 10:4–5 that knowing God is the weapon we use in warfare, and false arguments are one of the things that hinder us from knowing God. A false argument, such as: God's love is conditional.

1 Corinthians 13:4–8 speaks of what love is and is not. The love used in those scriptures is *agapé*, the noun form of the word "love". Now that we know that noun form is actually God, fill in the blanks below with the word God.

"_____ is patient, _____ is kind. _____ does not envy, _____ does not boast, _____ is not proud. _____ does not dishonor others, _____ is not self-seeking, _____ is not easily angered, _____ keeps no record of wrongs. _____ does not delight in evil but rejoices with the truth. _____ always protects, always trusts, always hopes, always perseveres. _____ never fails." (1 Cor. 13:4–8)

This is who God *is*. This is whom He is asking you to trust, and this is the faithful stronghold He desires you to take refuge in. Scripture declares:

> God is not a man, so he does not lie. He is not human, so he does not change his mind. Has he ever spoken and failed to act? Has he ever promised and not carried it through? (Num. 23:19)

We can trust what we've learned here today to never change. We do not need to live a suspicious life toward God. We do not need to stay guarded before the Lord. We are safe to open wide our hearts and trust that whatever He wants to do in there is to make us more and more like Him.

Before you move on, close your eyes and imagine how big our God is. Allow Him to bring to you the revelation of His love for you personally. Don't rush this. It's only about you and Him right now. Stay in this place until you feel the Spirit release you to move on. Allow the sweetness of His presence to consume every part of you.

Love Is a Stronghold

Our counterfeit stronghold is literally destroyed by the love that flows from the authentic stronghold. And my friend, if God is love then love is a stronghold. The doorway to your freedom is opened by one thing—His love. The more His love remains in you, then God will reproduce himself in you, right up to the point His love overflows to others. ". . . God lives in us, and his love is brought to full expression in us" (1 John 4:12).

The only way for us to love like God loves is to allow the full expression of His love to grow within us. Then, and only then, are we able to express 2 Corinthians 13:4–8 to a dying world!

> *Oh God, forgive us for making you so small in our eyes. God you are limitless, and we cannot fully comprehend the magnitude of your love for us. Dying on the cross was enough, yet now you've given us a fresh revelation of the width, depth, length, and height of your love. I pray, Father, that we never again allow guilt and shame to keep us from your presence, from your unfailing love. Never again allow us to buy a lie that your love is conditional.*
>
> *In Jesus' name, Amen.*

Journal Your Journey

P.S. An after thought . . .

- Go back in your journal where you wrote what loves means to you. Is there anything you'd like to change about that?

- Then go back to our key scripture, and write what speaks to you about that scripture in light of knowing who God is.

CHAPTER 4

Take Captive
Those Thoughts

I prayed to the LORD, and he answered me.
He freed me from all my fears.
Psalm 34:4

The phone rang. My husband's doctor was on the other end. Ten days earlier he had gone in for a biopsy that the doctor wasn't concerned about. It was a better safe than sorry type of procedure—neither of us worried.

Everything beyond the words "it's malignant" seemed to become a faint echo in the background as the blood rushed from my head to my feet. While life around me suddenly began to move in slow motion, the thoughts in my head were flipping though my mind like a slideshow on rapid release!

Did he just say it's cancer?
Breathe.
Focus, and ask questions.

Breathe.
Hold it together.
Breathe.

Stunned by the news, I slowly set the phone on the counter and slid down my kitchen wall to the floor. My body was not responding to my mind. I wanted to cry, but the shock left me in disbelief. I wanted to run, but I couldn't get up off the kitchen floor. Everything in time and space stood still—everything, that is, but my mind. Fear just wouldn't stop talking. Question after question was released into the atmosphere of my mind, and every answer had a devastating ending.

We needed a stronghold. We stood before God as a family whose seams needed to be hedged, or else we were liable to come unraveled. Could God be trusted? Would Tom die? How would the bills be paid? How would the children navigate cancer? Would our marriage survive? These are the questions my fear wanted to answer, but my spirit was longing to hear from the One. Would He answer me?

As the days passed, I was locked in a fortress of fear. It resided in the deep caverns of my spirit where doubt joins forces with anxiety to produce an ugly concoction of panic. I kept it all locked away in my thoughts. Now more than ever Tom needed a woman of faith. Nevertheless my thoughts, when left unchecked, wildly interpreted the unknown with suffocating fear. My eyes were dictating my hope, and I believed what I could see. Only the known was my compass, and faith for the unseen seemed too high a risk to take. Reality was forcing my hand to deal with what was known, and turning my fear into its best friend.

One afternoon, I had just paid the bills, and the stress of our finances collided with what little faith remained. Without Tom working it would be impossible to make ends meet. So I mentally began to make arrangements for our family once we lost the house and car. Hopeless and dazed, I stared at the artwork hanging above our couch. There in the photo, a man stood before the half-opened door of a lighthouse, and behind him an enormous and unexpected wave was engulfing him and the entire house. I whispered to God, "Our family is that man, and this cancer is that wave."

Without hesitation, He instantly spoke to my spirit: *then step into the lighthouse.* I walked over to the picture and touched the frame, as if in some way I was touching God. I read aloud the scripture engraved below.

The LORD is my rock, my fortress, and my savior;
my God is my rock, in whom I find protection.
He is my shield, the power that saves me, and my place of safety.
Psalm 18:2

Our family may have been that man, and the cancer may have been that wave, but God was that lighthouse. As I declared aloud the scripture, instantaneously my fear of the unknown vanished, and it was like faith came up for air again! God didn't answer my questions asked in fear, because God doesn't speak to fear. He speaks to faith. He instantly answered my faithful cry for help, delivered me from a fortress of fear, and set me into His stronghold.

The Power of the Mind

The brain is a powerful tool and a mighty weapon. It has the ability to launch people into a literal outer space or shut them down in a figurative abyss. Dr. Caroline Leaf, communications pathologist and audiologist states,

> Your mind is a switch. You have an extraordinary ability to determine, achieve, and maintain optimal levels of intelligence, mental health, peace, and happiness, as well as prevention of disease in your body and mind. *You can, through conscious effort, gain control of your thoughts and feelings.* In doing so you can change the programming and chemistry of your brain.[1]
>
> —*Switch On Your Brain*, emphasis mine

As I stood before that picture on the wall, my encounter with God literally flipped a switch in my brain. God presented me with a choice: stay outside the lighthouse and let the wave consume you, or step in and allow the safety of the stronghold to protect you. I had the power to choose.

The fear of cancer was dictating every decision I was making, taking away my right to choose. When God confronted me, and showed me I had a choice, I felt empowered again. Neither my fear nor my faith had the power to control my free will. Only I had that authority, and God was reminding me to use it. When I responded by stepping into His stronghold, my decision altered the entire journey of Tom's cancer. What could have been a season walked in insurmountable fear had been replaced with indescribable faith. My decision to believe for what I could not see, Tom later shared, gave him the faith to believe too. My faith infected the entire family. When our children were fearful, we stood as a covering of faith for them.

Throughout this chapter, we will talk about taking captive our thoughts and aligning them to the will of God. We will discuss how the choice of our declaration influences our actions, and our actions will determine our destination. We will also expose the lies laced with truth, and confirm our authority to capture those rebellious thoughts and teach them to obey Christ.

The "Suddenlies" of Life

The definition of suddenly is "quickly and unexpectedly". Our lives are carved with a series of sudden moments, like the loss of a job, divorce, illness, or death. These moments leave permanent spots on our lives.

> For man does not know his time. Like fish that are
> taken in an evil net, and like birds that are caught in
> a snare, so the children of man are snared at an evil
> time, when it suddenly falls upon them. (Eccl. 9:12)

Interview 100 different people, and you will find 100 different life-altering moments that formed their lives. The Grand Canyon National Park has layers upon layers of etched earth and rock from the rise and fall of water levels that have moved soil and stone for centuries. Our minds are like that canyon but on an even grander scale. And our sufferings, trials, and out-of-our-control moments move the river that shapes and redefines the landscape of our lives. My husband's cancer was in that river, and it reshaped our family's life.

Journal Your Journey

- Take a moment and ask the Lord to reveal to you the "suddenlies" in your life that have altered the landscape of your mind.

Our Declarations Determine Our Actions

How we respond to these sudden moments in our life influences the outcome of our faith. Ultimately it will lead us down a road, either closer or farther away from the presence of God.

> Today I have given you the choice between life and death, between blessings and curses. Now I call on heaven and earth to witness the choice you make. Oh, that you would choose life, so that you and your descendants might live! (Deut. 30:19)

We are faced with a choice, and when we do not choose faith then by default we are choosing to react in fear. To stand in fear grants the enemy entrance into our life, and allows him to move freely about our events. When we make a choice to stand in faith, we give God complete access to our life, and the authority to move on our behalf.

In Acts 16:16–26, Paul and Silas were on their way to a prayer meeting when they unexpectedly encountered a demon-possessed fortuneteller. The woman followed Paul and Silas for days, shouting at them. In exasperation Paul turned to her and cast the demon out of her. The woman's master, now without the ability to make money, grabbed Paul and Silas and brought them before the marketplace authorities. A mob quickly formed against Paul and Silas. They were stripped, beaten, and thrown into prison. While Paul and Silas were in prison, they began praying and praising God. *Suddenly* there was an earthquake, the prison doors flew open, and the chains of every prisoner broke off.

Each time, Paul and Silas chose to respond in faith to the sudden moment they encountered. When they ran into the woman who began shouting and taunting them, they exercised their faith and cast the demon out of the woman in the name of Jesus. When they were stripped, beaten, and thrown into prison, they chose to engage their faith by praising and worshiping God in their chains. When our default is faith, it positions us to encounter a "suddenly" moment from God.

When we encounter a "suddenly" from God, people are released from their chains. The apostles' faith in God set the possessed woman free, and loosed the chains of the prisoners. While Tom was going through treatment, our decision of faith didn't just carry us, but it carried others too. We received letters, cards, and stories from people in our church, and friends and family, who shared that by seeing us endure in faith, it gave them the faith to persevere too. Faith is contagious, and each time we choose to respond to life by the power of the word of God, we infect others. Likewise, our thoughts that do not align with the word of God have equal power to influence and infect those around us.

Take Captive Our Thoughts

Second Corinthians 10:5 says, "We capture their rebellious thoughts and teach them to obey Christ." We possess the ability to capture a thought that opposes the word of God, and then teach it to obey the Word. In order to teach something, we must know it. Otherwise, we teach it incorrectly. Sometimes a lie feels like a truth simply because it sounds logical, or we've heard it repeated over the years. Logic and popular rhetoric do not make something truthful.

Our thoughts can trick us. For example, I've heard "God, helps those who help themselves" quoted as a Bible verse. People will align their thoughts to a false teaching because it's been spoken over and over and seems logical—when in reality it's a false teaching. The truth of the Word is, "For you have been a stronghold to the poor, a stronghold to the needy in his distress. . ." (Isa. 25:4 ESV). According to scripture, God helps the helpless. Here are some of our thoughts in contrast to the God's word.

OUR THOUGHTS	GOD'S WORD	BIBLE VERSE
"It's impossible"	"All things are possible"	Luke 18:27
"I'm too tired"	"I will give you rest"	Matthew 11:28-30
"Nobody really loves me"	"I love you"	John 3:16, 34
"I can't go on"	"My grace is sufficient"	2 Corinthians 12:9
"I can't figure things out"	"I will direct your steps"	Proverbs 3:5-6
"I can't do it"	"You can do all things"	Philippians 4:13
"I'm not able"	"I am able"	2 Corinthians 9:8
"It's not worth it"	"It will be worth it"	Romans 8:28
"I can't forgive myself"	"I forgive you"	1 John 1:9
"I can't manage"	"I will supply all your needs"	Philippians 4:19
"I'm afraid"	"I have not given you a spirit of fear"	2 Timothy 1:7
"I'm not smart enough"	"I give you wisdom"	1 Corinthians 1:30
"I feel all alone"	"I will never leave you or forsake you"	Hebrews 13:5

Journal Your Journey

- List in your journal some of the thoughts you may have aligned with and look up the scripture.

- Write out the scriptures that are truth against the lies you've believed.

- Choose the one that stands out the most and record it on either a 3x5 card, sticky note, or the home screen of your phone.

- Place the card or sticky note in a place you frequent in order to meditate on that scripture.

Our Declaration

Paul reminds us in 2 Corinthians 10:3 that the battle can only be fought in the Spirit, because it's not a physical one but a mental one. How is a battle of the mind waged?

In Matthew 4:1–11, Jesus faced Satan who attempted to take Him captive, cause Him to reject God, and submit His allegiance to the devil. Every time Satan would speak to Him, Jesus used the only weapon that holds the power to defeat the devil—the word of God. Three times the devil tempted Jesus and three times Jesus fought him with scripture. The devil departed when he realized Jesus could not be tempted. James 4:7 says, "Humble yourself before God, resist the devil, and he will leave you." The enemy cannot stand for any length of time against the word of God. We may have to quote the Word more than once, but eventually, like Jesus, the enemy will leave us alone.

When we declare the word of God in opposition to our feelings, thoughts, or the lies we've believed, we are activating 2 Corinthians 10:3–5. We are fighting the counterfeit stronghold through the power of the authentic stronghold.

> We are human, but we don't wage war as humans do. We use God's mighty weapons, not worldly weapons, to knock down the strongholds of human reasoning and to destroy false arguments. We destroy every proud obstacle that keeps people from knowing God. We capture their rebellious thoughts and teach them to obey Christ. (2 Cor. 10:3–5)

I can remember one day when I literally wrote on my hand James 1:20 "The wrath of man does not produce the righteousness of God." Every time I felt my anger rise that day, I would look down at my hand and quote the scripture out loud. When it was declared, my thoughts would align with the word of God, and my actions would then respond to my declarations.

What happens when we can't discern whether it's God's Word or not?

Discerning a Lie Cloaked in Truth

Sometimes a lie is cloaked within a scripture that's been misrepresented, and we cannot see the lie. For example, "The temptations in your life are no different from what others experience. And God is faithful. He will not allow the temptation to be more than you can stand. When you are tempted, he will show you a way out so that you can endure" (1 Cor. 10:13). This scripture is often misquoted as "God will not give you more than what you can handle." The scripture is clearly talking about temptation and not generalized challenges in life. People hear something misquoted over and over again, and begin to believe the misrepresented scripture as a truth. Then in this situation when faced with difficulties far greater than they can bear, the scripture become fallacious. Jesus said, a little yeast spoils the bread; well, a twist of the Word voids it of truth. A twisted scripture can corrode our spirits, and without warning we can find ourselves in a stronghold of deception.

Genesis 2:16–18 and 3:1–13 are perfect examples of a lie being cloaked within scripture.

Journal Your Journey

Read Genesis 2:16–18 and 3:1–13 in your Bible.
Answer the following:

- What was the command for the trees?
  (Genesis 2:16–17)

- Was Eve there when the command was given?
  (Genesis 2:18)

- How is the serpent described? (Genesis 3:1)

- Did Eve recognize the first lie the serpent told?
  (Genesis 3:2)

- Did Eve quote God's command correctly back to the
  enemy? (Genesis 3:3)

- Did Eve recognize the second lie the serpent told?
  (Genesis 3:6)

- What did Eve confess to the Lord? (Genesis 3:13)

Adam received the command from God firsthand, and
the serpent didn't go after Adam; he went after the one
who had secondhand knowledge of the word of God. Eve
hadn't encountered the word of God for herself. She'd only
received it from someone else. When she quoted God's
word back to the serpent, she quoted it incorrectly. The
serpent realized Eve didn't possess firsthand knowledge
of the word of God, thus Eve was an easy target to be de-

ceived. The enemy is looking for secondhand consumers of the word of God so he can be a firsthand deceiver.

Our primary consumption of the word of God cannot come from a secondary source. Pastors, friends, and group leaders are all great supplements to a daily personal consumption to the word of God, but if used as the primary source, we're carrying around a substandard weapon. Then we're at risk of doing exactly what Eve did; we will expose our vulnerabilities toward the enemy through our lack of knowledge.

When we quote an incorrect scripture in battle it magnifies our vulnerabilities. It's like raising a toy sword and plastic shield to the enemy. The devil knows God's Word. He was there when it was written. He saw it spoken into existence. He knows how to interpret it, and he recognizes it being misinterpreted. However, the enemy is powerless to know your thoughts. He cannot read your mind; therefore, he will test you and see if you are someone who carries the Word as a firsthand or secondhand consumer. Do not allow the enemy to outsmart you with the word of God. Feed yourself and know your Word.

Discerning a Lie Cloaked in Fact

Deception is found not just in the church; it seeps into every part of our life. Today many laws of government are fashioned in direct opposition to the laws of God, and scientific theories are believed as fact because people do not know their Word.

Many of us come with a family history of mental and emotional illnesses, even drug and alcohol abuse. It is a scientific fact that genetics and environmental influencers are predispositions to be a leading factor in those who suffer from such things. These proofs would make it easy to believe our destiny is the destiny of those who have gone before us. So careless comments, misleading quotes, laws and well-meaning educational information aid in the deception and cloud our discernment when the voice of the enemy whispers,

"You'll turn out just like your mother."
"You can't beat this. No one has beaten this disease."
"You're destined to die, just like your father died."

Lies. Friend, unless you know the word of God firsthand you will believe these warped lies as though they were fact. Dr. Caroline Leaf says,

> Taken collectively, the studies on epigenetics show us that the good, the bad, and the ugly do come down through the generations, but your mind is the signal—the epigenetic factor—that switches these genes on or off. *Therefore, you are not destined to live out the negative patterns of your forbearers—you can instead make a life choice to overcome by tweaking their patterns of expression.*[2]
>
> —*Switch On Your Brain*, emphasis mine

75

Testimony of Truth
Grace's Story:

> As far back as I can remember my father suffered from anxiety and depression. When I was a child I didn't know those words. All I saw was that he was sad, constantly worried, isolated, and he never hugged me or said, "I love you." It wasn't until I got older and started feeling and acting similar to him that I learned what the words anxiety and depression meant, and how they related to me.
>
> I didn't grow up in a very nurturing or loving home, and the church I was raised in was spiritually abusive. I fell into the same emotional pattern of my father. My world seemed to be defined by depressed and anxious thoughts, and I felt stuck. I turned to my mother for comfort and hope, but she spoke words over me like "This is normal." and "You're just like your dad." My fate seemed cemented that this is how I would always feel. As I grew older the depression and anxiety became worse. Eventually, I was put on antidepressants because I was suicidal.
>
> As a Christian, those feelings didn't make any sense to me. I should be powerful, faith-filled, and hopeful. Nevertheless, that was not the case, and I felt paralyzed by my fears.

Coming from a spiritually abusive background, I struggled with shame, because I felt hopeless, afraid, and lonely. The shame prompted me to control my surroundings, and to fix my circumstances and myself.

Instead of turning to God for guidance I made my choices based on my own emotions, hoping to prove my worth to Him. Inevitably, those choices led to trials and struggles. Relying on my own strength to overcome became my normal response.

I was afraid to trust God, because I believed the lies my sin and shame were telling me. The lies told me I couldn't be accepted for who I was and what I had become. Continually my mind was being attacked, and before I knew it, I spiraled so low that I even questioned my salvation.

As I cried out to Him, begging for forgiveness, I will never forget how He responded to me. He asked me to give Him ALL of me. He wasn't just asking me to surrender my successes, He asked me to surrender my failures. The very things that made me feel inadequate and unworthy of His love. In return for surrendering my struggles, He extended mercy, grace, and loving kindness toward me. In that moment, I felt complete acceptance and love from my heavenly Father in a way I had never experienced before.

77

I realized my fate was not to live like my father, anxious and depressed. My fate was to swim in the ocean of God's never-ending grace and love, where my sin and shame were washed away, and the blood of Jesus supernaturally gave me what I didn't deserve—peace, purity, and righteousness.

Whenever an anxious or lying thought creeps up on me, I choose to surrender those thoughts to the Lord. The more I surrender to Him and trust in Him, the more I become like Him. As I open myself to Him I begin to reflect Him, my thoughts and actions align with His kingdom, and peace becomes my portion.

We have the power to influence our own destiny. The enemy does not get to dictate what our future looks like, because the enemy isn't privileged to anyone's future but his own. Only God knows our destiny, and the word of God says our destiny is good.

> For we are God's masterpiece. He has created us anew in Christ Jesus, so we can do the good things he planned for us long ago. (Eph. 2:10)

God planned good things; the word good is agathos in the Greek. It describes what originates from God and what is empowered through Him. We are the masterpieces God designed to accomplish such things. The enemy knows the beautiful destinies connected to God's masterpieces, because he was once one of them. But he gave up his destiny. Now his mission is to have you give yours up too. He will stop at nothing to limit your influence and derail your destiny. He also knows if you become a firsthand consumer of the word of God, you will become unstoppable.

Journal Your Journey

- Write in your journal the top three lies you have believed.

- As you spend time in His presence this week, consider the lies and ask for scriptural truths to defeat them.

- Commit to being a firsthand consumer of the word of God.

God Determines Our Identity

Be alert and on guard so that you do not to take on another person's bondage as your identity. You've been given your very own in Christ. My dear friend, like Grace, you are not a diagnosis. You are not your past. You are not the black sheep of the family. You are not destined to live out your parents' life. You are a new creation in Christ. "This means that anyone who belongs to Christ has become a new person. The old life is gone; a new life has begun!" (2 Cor. 5:17).

As a new creation, you have been set apart to fulfill a new destiny, not an old family curse. You are designed to share in God's glory. "You can be sure of this: The Lord set apart the godly for himself. The Lord will answer when I call to him." (Ps. 4:3).

Since you share in His glory, you are not filled with a disease; you are filled with His spirit. Your mind and body exhibit the glory of the Lord. "Don't you realize that all of you together are the temple of God and that the Spirit of God lives in you?" (1 Cor. 3:16).

Your depression does not determine your future. Your anxiety does not say where you'll go. Your parents' mistakes do not get to design your future family, and your emotions do not get to rule your days. "And having chosen them, he called them to come to him. And having called them, he gave them right standing with himself. And having given them right standing, he gave them his glory." (Rom. 8:30).

Your emotions may spill over for a day, but they do not get to consume your world. The same Spirit that told the oceans where to stop and it determined the force of the wind resides in you. You hold that power now. "He established the force of the wind and measured out the waters." (Job 28:25).

Out of the Heart

It is the "suddenlies" of our life that expose what's in our heart and how we perceive ourselves. What is in our heart becomes our default declaration, and our declaration will determine our destination. God has given us the power to choose our responses. His Word gives us the ability to use truth as a shield for our heart, so that the enemy doesn't take our suddenlies and use them as sudden-lies to throw us off course.

Proverb 4:23 says, "Guard your heart above all else, for it determines the course of your life." The word of God is the stronghold for our hearts, protecting it against attack. The scriptures are designed as both an offensive and defensive weapon against the father of lies, the devil. We can ensure our default declarations are like those of Paul instead of those of Eve, by becoming firsthand consumers of what it contains. Then we hold the power, like Paul, to be released from our captivity, and guide other prisoners to freedom.

> *Father, we submit our minds to you. We ask that you cleanse them of any lies that we've believed. Father, we long to know your Word and your ways better. We want your truth entwined in our DNA. Father, draw us deeper than we've ever gone before. Give us a hunger for the Word like never before. Do not allow us to be satisfied with a secondhand knowledge of scripture. Teach us to*

feed ourselves from your Word. We declare as our scripture, Jeremiah 33:3, "Call to me and I will answer you, and will tell you great and hidden things that you have not known." to position us to receive a fresh revelation of your Word.

In Jesus' name, amen.

CHAPTER 5

Bondage of Busyness

He who dwells in the shelter of the Most High, will rest in the shadow of the Almighty.

Psalm 91:1

Our journey through the past four chapters has brought us revelation that God is the authentic stronghold, and through the work of the cross we have the power to overcome the pull of sin. We've also discovered that our worth does not dictate His love, and that the word of God is the stronghold for the heart. However, not every battle in our mind comes from sin, shame, or painful childhood memories. Sometimes the battle in the mind is a conflict of priorities and how we should invest our time. We can be certain any time we are conflicted that the enemy is poised for attack.

More Than Enough to Do

We live in a world of countless prospects, and priorities play an important role in the welfare of our mind, body, and spirit. Lysa TerKeurst writes, "The decisions you make today matter. Every decision points your life in the direction you are about to travel. No decision is an isolated choice. It's a chain of events."[1] As believers, mishandling our priorities can trigger a chain of events that lead us into the bondage of busyness. Socrates warns, "Beware of the barrenness of a busy life," and rightfully so. There is no shortage of opportunities to serve others in church, our children's schools, our jobs, or our communities. Jesus said, "the harvest is plentiful but the workers are few." We can find ourselves pouring into all of these open doors and opportunities and end up feeling depleted.

The Bible describes believers as a body connected together. We are wired to serve and live connected with a purpose. We are also created to worship, and if we are not worshiping God we will substitute something else to worship instead of Him—our career, our title, our family, and our church. The enemy will exploit our design and entrap us in a cycle of doing for others, and we can confuse serving, even in the church, as being with God.

My children are now driving themselves and planning for college, but the days of a neverending to-do list that revolved around their lives and homeschooling are not too far removed. The moment my feet would hit the ground, I was responding to the loudest bidder for my immediate attention. The night before, I would purpose to wake up before the family and begin my day at the feet of Jesus, but somewhere between my snooze button and the firstborn's alarm going off, the magnetic pull between my head and the pillow did not release.

As a young mom, I understood in my head that time with the Lord was my go-juice; it just seemed expendable when everything else required an instant response. I would divert my quiet time to my service to others and go about my day. After all, I would be leading my small group that night, and participating in several meetings as the kids church director, and the women's ministry leader, and don't forget prayer at 6:00 p.m. Surely, I was with God.

The more I served, the less I spent time with Him. The less time I spent alone with God, the more irritable, impatient, and self-absorbed I became. It didn't take long for my outlook on life to darken. I felt often like everyone wanted a piece of me, and I couldn't meet the needs of the crowd. I thought what I was doing was God's will—isn't that what was expected as a wife, mom, and believer? If so, why was I feeling so depleted and longing for rest?

God's Order

A few ugly meltdowns, by me not the kids, gave the clue it was time to reevaluate my life. I was unhappy, my family was unhappy, and we are *Christians*—we're supposed to be happy people! My spiritual mom, Jeanie, sat and listened to my woes. She smiled, pulled out her pen and said, "Daughter, your life is out of order." I thought, no kidding, mom. On a simple piece of white paper she scribbled down God's order for our life. It was like Moses getting the Ten Commandments. She explained to me that God designed our lives so that He would remain at the top. Not in a way that He would lord over us, but so everything we did would flow from the original source of life—God. It was remarkable. She went on to explain that my standards as a wife, mother, servant, and employee would never be achieved outside of this order.

In that moment, I realized that regardless of how organized I was, if my day didn't start at the feet of Jesus, embracing the presence of His Holy Spirit, I would end my day feeling as though I fell short, again, because my standard was set outside of His grace.

> But he said to me, "My grace is sufficient for you, for my power is made perfect in weakness." Therefore I will boast all the more gladly about my weaknesses, so that Christ's power may rest on me. (2 Cor. 12:9 NIV)

Most of my days left me feeling defeated, and I knew I needed His power. The Lord impressed upon my heart that the gap between His strength and my weakness had always been filled by His grace. Every time I hit the mark in motherhood or any other part of my life, it was by His grace. Knowing how my order likened to His was the only way to understand where the breakdown happened. I set the list Jeanie drew before me, it was time I tried to make sense of my messy chaotic life. I compared God's order to mine and it exposed why my life was devoid His power and was exhausting me of mine.

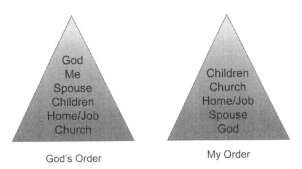

God's Order · My Order

Wow! I was far more out of order than I realized. God's design is a lot like the champagne stack at a wedding. It starts with a large base of glasses and then row after row of delicate glass is stacked upon that base until there is only one glass at the top. The champagne is then poured into the single glass, and out of the overflow of that single glass everything else is filled. My life was far from overflowing. I didn't even have the single glass sitting at the top of the stack, and the champagne was nowhere in sight. No wonder my home was upside down and my marriage was strained.

Journal Your Journey

- In your journal, list God's order.

- Next list the order of your life.

- Compare the two and write out a prayer asking for wisdom and a strategy to align the two.

The most profound thing I learned that day was not how out of order my life was, but how serving the church and ministering to God is not quite the same. The first ministry I am responsible for is my ministry to God, and my first mission fields are my marriage and children. How I steward them defines the ministries and mission fields to come.

Ministering to God

You may be thinking, minister? I am not a pastor. Or, I thought pastors were called to minister to people, not God.

The verb form of *minister* is to take care of the needs of someone. As a body of believers in Christ we are called to take care of the needs of one another and those around us (see Eph. 4:16; Matt. 28:19). However, we are also called to minister to the Lord. Watchman Nee, who was like a twentieth century Apostle Paul said, "Many of you are doing your utmost to help your brethren, and you are laboring to save sinners and administer the affairs of the church. But let me ask you: Have you been seeking to meet the need around you, or have you been seeking to serve the Lord?" In other words, serving the body and ministering to the needs of others is God's design, but to minister to others without it coming from a place of first ministering to God makes us idolaters. Exodus 20:3 says not to put anything above God—not even ministry.

Jeff Goins writes:

> To "minister to the Lord" is to worship him alone in all that you do. So, in essence, any ministry that is directed towards others without first being directed towards God is idolatry. There is a passage in Ezekiel 44 that describes two types of Levites (those who were in charge of taking care of the Jewish Temple—the place of worship). One group was ministering to the temple—that is, they were upholding religious practices while worshiping idols in their hearts. The other group was ministering directly to the Lord, honoring him as holy, and obeying him with their hearts. Concerning the first group, God says, "You brought foreigners uncircumcised in heart and flesh into my sanctuary, desecrating my temple while you offered me food, fat and blood, and you broke my covenant" (v. 7 NIV). Even though they made offerings to God, he didn't accept them, because they were being hypocritical by not glorifying God with their whole lives.[2]

Although we are not Levites, the Bible does call us a royal priesthood (see 1 Pet. 2:9). We are commanded to keep God first, and to offer ourselves to God as a living sacrifice. The Bible says it is our purest form of worship (see Rom. 12:1).

If we serve people out of obligation, if we say yes to an opportunity, hoping to impress a pastor or leader, or if we put ourselves out there hoping to be seen by others, it's like the Levites who ministered to the temple, but their hearts were given to idols. Ministering and serving with any motive other than to love God is serving with a divided heart.

Everything seen on the list Jeanie drew out for me is a form of ministry to God—meeting the needs of others, which is in turn meeting the needs of the Lord. Watchman Nee also said, "Let us note at the outset that there is little apparent difference between ministry to the House of the Lord and ministry to the Lord Himself." The only difference is the heart motive behind it. It's only ministry to God after we've been to the Lord's throne room. Apart from that it's idolatry.

When I first heard the term "ministering to God", my initial thought was: How? What does it even mean? Do I have to work in a church? Do I have to start a ministry? What are His needs?

How Do We Minister to God?

Since today there are no Levitical temple duties to fulfill, we minister to the Lord by serving our community, helping the poor and orphaned, and taking a responsible role in our home church. Another aspect of ministering to the Lord is going before His throne in:

- Prayer

- Worship

- Studying the word of God

Entering into the throne room of God is sort of like being invited over to His home. It's here where we engage in building our relationship with Him. Here is where the overflow of our heart meets the overflow of His.

Some might say, "But I already do that." And you may. For that I give you two thumbs up. The important part of ministering to God this way is our heart motive. If prayer, worship, and studying the Word are just parts of a daily checklist, then our attempts at ministering to the Lord are no more than religious responses, and He rejects them. However, if they are a form of creating a deeper relationship with Him, then our offerings please Him. "Live a life filled with love, following the example of Christ. He loved us and offered himself as a sacrifice for us, a pleasing aroma to God" (Eph. 5:2). When we offer our time to God in this way, it's sacrificial, and becomes a pleasing aroma to Him. Our time set apart for Him then fills our lives with the love we talked about in Chapter Three.

Our prayer time, worship, and studying the word of God were never designed to be a quick prayer before we get out of bed, a worship song on the way to work, or a devotional sent to our email. While some days those are the best we can do, and God's grace covers days like that, they are not the ministries due our King. Let's go a little deeper into the ways we can minister to the Lord.

Prayer

There are many types of prayers; I don't believe one is preferred above the other. The most important part is the transparent heart before the Lord. David said, "Search me, O God, and know my heart; test me and know my anxious thoughts" (Ps. 139:23). We do not have to choose one prayer at a time; we can incorporate all in one setting.

- Thanksgiving–*gratitude and declarations of God's goodness*

- Confession–*acknowledging we messed up and are repentant*

- Supplication or requests–*seeking guidance, healing, safety, blessing*

- Meditative/Contemplative–*waiting upon the Lord, meditative, contemplative, and centering prayer.*

Note: When we wait, we are neither speaking nor being spoken to, but resting in the glorious presence of God, completely engulfed in His love. Some call this "soaking".

Journal Your Journey

Choose one type of prayer and focus for 5–10 minutes. Journal about your experience after you are finished.

- What feelings did you experience toward God?

- What are some of the discoveries you made while in prayer?

- How did the presence of God feel?

- Were there any challenges during your focused time?

Worship

Although the Bible speaks of many different ways to worship, the actions of worship are not what God desires—it's the heart behind the actions. John 4:24 commands, "For God is Spirit, so those who worship him must worship in spirit and in truth." When in worship it is easy to simultaneously worship in all types of ways, but here are three ways to worship.

- Praise and thanksgiving–*through a grateful declaration*

- Songs–*through singing songs and reading psalms*

- Dancing–*by kicking up your heels and dancing before the Lord*

93

Journal Your Journey

Choose one type of worship and focus for 5–10 minutes. Journal about your experience after you are finished.

- What feelings did you experience toward God?

- What are some of the discoveries you made while in worship?

- How did the presence of God feel?

- Were there any challenges during your focused time?

Study of the Word

A simple Google search will show you a variety of ways to study the Bible. The most important thing is to allow the word of God to be absorbed not just in your mind but also by your spirit. Second Timothy 2:15 states, "Study to show yourself approved to God, a workman that needs not to be ashamed, rightly dividing the word of truth" (AKJV).

The SOAP method is a common method to study scripture:

- Scripture–*Copy a verse.*

- Observation–*Write what stood out in the verse and what it means to you?*

- Application–*How can the scripture be applied?*

- Prayer–*Write out a prayer asking God to help you apply this verse today.*

Journal Your Journey

Focus for 5–10 minutes on studying one verse.
Journal about your experience after you are finished.

- What feelings did you experience toward God?

- What are some of the discoveries you made while in study?

- How did the presence of God feel?

- Were there any challenges during your focused time?

In God's order, the way we meet the needs of others is from the overflow of ministering to Him first. The Holy Spirit is like the champagne I spoke about, and we are like the single glass at the top of the stack. We are called to be an offering poured out before the Lord (see Rom. 12:1). We cannot pour out what we do not have. As we spend time with Him, He fills us up. The longer we remain, the more full in Him we become. The character traits of God, the word of God, the healing power of God, and the knowledge of God overflow out of us, and our lives become like that stack of champagne glasses. Everything under us will be filled from the source of One.

I challenge you to a 30/30. Take 30 minutes of your day for the next 30 days. Commit to ministering to the Lord through prayer, worship, and study for 30 minutes, before you commit to ministering in any other way. I promise that by the end of the 30 days, your discernment will be heightened, your focus will be on point, and your relationship with the Lord will be taken to an entirely new level. Oh, and by the end of the challenge you'll be looking for more than 30 minutes.

God's order is listed vertically, but often we fulfill some ministries simultaneously. There were days my house and kids came at the exact same time. When looking at God's order, it's important to see how it works for your family. The order doesn't change, but each person's abilities to fulfill them, whether simultaneously or individually, vary based on their personality, family dynamics, and physical stamina. I have missionary friends whose entire lives— children, homeschool, and marriages—are lived out on the mission field. For their family, life is ministry. In our home, we were a military family, and Tom's job dictated much of our life and how we lived it. Long deployments created a single-parent home, so when my children were little I had to limit my outside commitments in order to maintain a biblical order inside the home. Too many church commitments or school committees left me disheveled and discontent, which then had me focusing on everything I didn't have together and comparing my life to those who (I perceived) did.

At times, saying no felt like I was missing out on an opportunity. I had to learn it was OK to say no, because saying no isn't my strength—saying yes is. I am a thinker, planner, and doer. I don't like to be left behind or out of the picture. I must confess there were days I threw a temper tantrum in my proverbial prayer closet because I wanted to say yes, but I said no instead. Nevertheless, learning my limitations, and the individual dynamics of our home, kept me out of the bondage of busyness. Having some breathing room in my life allowed me to keep my eyes on God. The result allowed me to accurately discern the traps of getting out of order when opportunities, open doors, and long-term commitments came my way. It also gave me margin to say yes to God when a God-opportunity presented itself.

The Comparison Trap

Through the years, I have followed a well-known women's speaker. I have listened to her preach about being a wife, mother and minister simultaneously. As she travels the world with her family, life and ministry seem to blend harmoniously for them. After hearing one of her messages, that women can do both, I recall agonizing over putting my speaking and teaching career on hold, as I homeschooled my children and got them raised. I legitimately felt like I had failed God and missed my window to fulfill what I felt He was calling me to do. I opened my heart to the trap of comparison. "Pay careful attention to your own work, for then you will get the satisfaction of a job well done, and you won't need to compare yourself to anyone else" (Gal. 6:4).

I confess, I was trapped. My heart was no longer ministering to the Lord, because my eyes were too busy idolizing another person's ministry. The moment I began comparing myself, I removed a protective covering over my heart and mind. I became instantly anxious and my spirit was suddenly opened up to a barrage of lies.

"You'll never speak."
"Your time passed."
"There is no room for you."
"You should have started earlier."
"You're insignificant."
"What could you possibly offer?"

The lies we spoke about in Chapter Four were taking control of my every thought. I was frozen. I began to believe what I was hearing. I admit I entertained those thoughts for more than a few days. Suddenly, how God designed our family and its purpose wasn't good enough. I wanted what someone else had. I completely disregarded the things the Lord had spoken to me for years because I allowed envy to grab hold of my heart. By comparing my life to that woman's life, I left my lane and stopped plowing my own field. I now wanted to plow hers. Maybe you've wandered out of your lane, and you desire the things in another person's life: a husband, a child, a career, or maybe a ministry. Maybe, like me, you absorbed a barrage of lies that left you feeling like it will never happen for you.

That feeling of *never* was the red flag to my spirit. It is the enemy who deals in fear-based absolutes, not God. When I realized the trap I had fallen into, I began quoting scripture, just like we learned in Chapter Four, and the enemy did exactly what the Word said he would do—he fled. The fear-based absolutes turned into faith-filled declarations of God's promises for my life. Comparing my family dynamics to that speaker's family dynamics was nothing more than an ugly swamp trap to draw me into condemnation and tempt me to do more than what I was called to do in that particular time of my life.

Journal Your Journey

- Are you caught in a comparison trap?

- Take time to journal about what you are comparing yourself to, and why you think you do this.

- What fear-based absolutes are you listening to?

- Write out some faith-filled declarations in response to them.

Trap Doors

A sneaky trap door of the enemy is to provide us the opportunity of a lifetime so we can walk into a counterfeit destiny. Not every open door is a door opened by the Lord. Even if that door looks like it leads to our dreams. The call comes in. The job offer opens up. The friend asks you to help her with a great project. It all seems so dreamy. Impulsively, without consulting God, we say yes. Of course we will add this opportunity to our plate. What's one more thing? It's the opportunity of a lifetime, and what if it never comes by again?

Then there is the revolving trap door. It's the one you wish would close, because you opened it out of obligation. Now, you are afraid to disappoint and it's just become a trap of your time, limiting you to what God has designed for you to do. Lysa TerKeurst states, "Whenever you say yes to something, there is less of you for something else. Make sure your yes is worth the less."

These trap doors are camouflaged in fear. We walk through them afraid the opportunity won't come again, and fearful that we will disappoint others. Or worse, it won't get done. The root of these fears is heard in the excuses why we cannot quit. They begins with "I'm afraid if . . ."

A woman who ministers to the Lord first will easily trust His timing and confidently say no to opportunities that pull her out of God's order for her life. She will resist the urge to live in a fear-based mindset of "what if." She will know that it's better to disappoint man than to disobey God, because she has learned God's character is to give us an abundant life filled with purpose, not an overly busy one filled with barreness.

> Be anxious for nothing, but in everything by prayer and supplication with thanksgiving let your requests be made known to God. And the peace of God, which surpasses all comprehension, will guard your hearts and your minds in Christ Jesus. (Phil. 4:6–7 NASB)

Philippians 4 is a perfect example of the overflow that comes from ministering to the Lord first. The word "peace" in the Greek is *eiréné* meaning peace of mind, and it comes from the root word *eiro*, "to join, to tie together in a whole". When we go before the Lord and submit our chaos, our anxiousness, our demands, and our dreams. He exchanges it all for His peace. That peace binds our minds together with the mind of Christ, pushing out any fear-based what ifs or absolutes, and makes us whole in Him. A woman whose life is submitted to God's order, who allows Him to ordain her steps, will behold a life joined with the mind of Christ. Our submission to His plan brings His peace, and that peace becomes the stronghold for our minds to rest within.

Journal Your Journey

- List in your journal the opportunities that have become your responsibilities.

- Write out any "I am afraid if..." responses to any of these responsibilities.

- Write out how the Lord would have you respond to those responsibilities.

Rest in the Lord

As women, when someone offers us the opportunity to rest, we usually respond with a gracious "I would like to, but . . . " In God's order, there is time for rest. God knew our nature wouldn't be to rest, so He made it a commandment. Carving out the 30/30 daily brings us before the throne of God, and there we rest. The throne room of God is His presence, and we have learned His presence is a shelter for the weary. Jesus called to the weary and said He would exchange their burdens for His and give them rest (see Matt. 11:28). And Psalm 91:1 says, "Whoever *dwells* in the shelter of the Most High will *rest* in the shadow of the Almighty" (NIV, emphasis mine).

In Hebrew the word "dwell" is *yashab*; "to sit, remain." The word "rest" is *luwn*; "to lodge, pass the night."

If we sit before the Lord ministering to Him first, He will invite us into a rest, a place to stay the night with Him. Friends, think about that: we don't typically invite strangers into our home to stay the night. The Lord is inviting you as His friend to come and sit, not rush the stay, but make a comfortable home in His presence. Ministering to the Lord first creates an intimate relationship with God the Son, a trusting relationship with God the Father, and a more in-tune relationship with God the Holy Spirit. The burden of busyness is designed to overwhelm our schedules and prevent us from carving out time to cultivate such a relationship. Without that relationship, we spend our lives striving, pushing, and positioning to be picked by a man, because we have forgotten we were chosen by a King.

We do not have to strive for the fulfillment of God's plan for our life. We do not have to be afraid that we will miss it. God will open doors that no one will be able to close. How we steward our first ministry will dictate the God-ordained open doors.

"Write this letter to the angel of the church in Philadelphia. This is the message from the one who is holy and true, the one who has the key of David. What he opens, no one can close; and what he closes, no one can open" (Rev. 3:7).

The key of David in the Old Testament (see Isa 22:22) represented the Gatekeeper, the one with the authority to control entry into the royal kingdom. As the king's steward, he would decide who could or could not have access to the king. In Isaiah it represented a prophetic illustration of Jesus, the one who now hold's the Key of David (see Rev 3:7) and controls the access into the Kingdom of Heaven and is the direct connection to God. It is by Christ alone that we can come boldly to the throne of our gracious God. Where we will receive his mercy and find help. In His throne room are the doors that open which no man can close.

The fear of what ifs and the barrenness of an overcommitted life can create panic in our minds. This fear can cause us to put more energy into the things we are afraid we will never have. Instead of investing in a relationship with the One who will effortlessly give to us our deepest desires. It is time we stop exerting unnecessary energy, and boldly go before His throne.

> If you then, being evil, know how to give good gifts to your children, how much more will your Father who is in heaven give what is good to those who ask Him! (Matt. 7:11 NASB)

Friend, maybe you sit holding an unfulfilled dream. Maybe you wonder if you will ever be married or pregnant. Maybe you use your busy schedule to keep God out of pain. Do not allow the busyness of life to distract you from the one who wants to answer all of those questions and fulfill all of those dreams. Our Father longs to rest your weary soul, and within that rest fulfill your deep longings.

Journal Your Journey

- List the longings you have in your heart.

- Write out a prayer surrendering those dreams and hopes.

- Commit in prayer to releasing your busy life and embracing a life of rest.

Father, today our eyes have been set upon you. Do not allow us to stray from our first call to ministry. Keep us tucked up under your wing. Grow in us a desire to know you more and to develop a trust like never before. Let your Word be a lamp unto our feet and guide our steps. Take the striving out of our days and replace it with the peace you have promised.

We pray this in Jesus' name, amen.

CHAPTER 6

Trust His Name

Those who know your name trust in you,
for you O Lord, do not abandon those who search for you.
Psalm 9:10

I was 13, and he was married with a little girl. I stayed very still in hopes he would go away, but he didn't. I was 14, and he was 18. I said no, and he said I didn't mean it. Silenced by shame and fear I stuffed the memories so deep, not even I could find them.

One out of every six women has been the victim of a sexual assault or abuse. At a staggering 17.7 million American women, that's over 10% of the female population in the United States, and studies show 93% of the victims know their attackers. I am one of those numbers—and with those odds, friend, it is safe to guess you might be one of them, too.[1]

Victims of sexual assault are three times more likely to suffer from depression. Six times more likely to suffer from Post Traumatic Stress Disorder. Thirteen times more likely to abuse alcohol, and 26 times more likely to abuse drugs. Women who have been assaulted are 4 times more likely to contemplate suicide.[2]

At 38 years old I was raging with anger and plummeting into depression. My journals are laced with pleading prayers for deliverance. As I shared in Chapter One, I didn't fully understand where my cry for help would take me, but I was about to learn. God was unearthing a secret I had forgotten I kept.

According to the American Association of Pastoral Care, there is conflicting research on how abused and non-abused women perceive God. Since the research is inconclusive, I am not going to tell you how to feel.[3] I am just going to share my story in hopes that as I open up it gives you permission to open up, too. Iyanla Vanzant says, "When you stand and share your story in an empowering way, your story will heal you and your story will heal somebody else."

It wasn't until my daughter turned 13 that the suppressed memories of my early teens surfaced. An absolutely terrifying moment, while watching a movie, unearthed a memory as if I was encountering it all over again for the very first time. My world froze, and the months to follow were walked out one desperate prayer after another.

I am not an expert in this area. I come to you standing as a confidant, a sister in arms, and one who has fought through the chaos in an attempt to make sense of what seemed so senseless. I had no idea my anger, need for control, and suspicious mindset were manifesting from a secret that was trying to release itself from the deepest parts of my soul.

If right now your heart is racing and you want to put the book down and never pick it back up, I understand that fear. The unknown is terrifying. Just hold on a little longer. I want you to know you're safe. I have your hand, we're going to walk together down this road, and then God will bring you another sister to take your hand and walk a little further—I promise.

Looking over my journals from 2008 I found this entry:

> Father, I'm scared of what I do not know. I know there is a hurt, something that happened to me when I was younger and I'm scared to look at it. I am scared to face whatever "it" was. Obviously it was traumatic enough that I buried it . . . I know it has developed this fear inside of me. Fear that has caused me to try and control every aspect of my life, and now there is this anger and rage taking over . . .

> *Beth, do not be afraid of the road you are on. I am bringing you through to set you free. Do not stop walking; do not be afraid of what you will see.*

> Habakkuk 3:19: "The Sovereign Lord is my strength! He makes me as surefooted as a deer and able to tread upon the heights."

> *Walk on, my daughter; do not stand still in fear of the cliff I have brought you near. Walk and advance to higher ground.*

109

A glimpse from the pages that hold some of the rawest moments of my life, show our fear is natural; we just cannot give it the power to rule us. If we allow it to hinder us from moving forward, then it turns from a reaction to a roadblock thwarting our freedom. The enemy's goal is to keep us so afraid of the unknown that we are willing to stay in the torment of the known. I was willing to stay in my torment because something inside of me didn't trust God or His Word. A battle had ensued deep in the caverns of my heart. A past where I felt powerless and violated was clashing with a God who was asking me to trust and surrender.

In the last two chapters we've talked about the importance of declaring the Word and knowing the Word, but what if we don't believe the Word? Unless we've had an authentic encounter with the presence of God, we cannot fully understand how the Word applies to our lives. I can write out scripture after scripture, but if I don't know it from experience, then I won't receive it. I had found myself declaring and believing for others, but when it came down to this area of my life God and I disconnected. Clearly I had some trust issues, and obviously He was going to deal with them.

As we've learned, what the Lord creates for our freedom, the enemy counterfeits for our destruction. The Lord's heart is to draw us into a deep and trusting relationship, whereas the enemy's plan is to distort or destroy that trust any way he can. We are most vulnerable to that with matters of the heart.

Intimacy with God

Throughout scripture God has used marriage and the close relationship between a man and a woman to describe the intimate relationship God has between His people and Himself. Throughout the New Testament Jesus refers to Himself as the bridegroom and the people of God as the bride. God has always planned to create a deep trusting relationship between Himself and mankind (1 Cor. 1:9). He started in the Garden with Adam and Eve. They walked naked and completely vulnerable before God. Both of them remained unashamed until sin came onto the scene.

Throughout the Bible there are many examples of such relationships to model. Abraham's relationship with God grew over the years until he trusted completely, and he was willing to sacrifice his child for Him, because He knew God would raise Him from the dead (see Gen. 22). Moses was so intimately connected to God that His glory shown upon his face (see Ex. 34:29). David trusted God so freely, he gave Him access to every area of his life: "Search me, O God, and know my heart; test me and know my anxious thoughts" (Ps. 139:23). These relationship examples show us how deeply we can know our God, and how profoundly intimate He desires it to be.

The Hebrew word for "know" is *yada*. It comes from the verb "to know." In the ancient language it was more than the idea of knowing, it actually described a more unconcealed understanding, and carried with it an intimate connection in the relationship such as Adam "knew" Eve sexually.

Jesus spoke of the same kind of "know" in the New Testament. The Greek word *ginóskó* is the type of intimate knowing experienced between a man and a woman. The Bible used the same word when Mary was confused about how she would be pregnant because said she did not "know" a man. These definitions of know come with a deep sense of vulnerability before the Lord.

Our definition of "know" is not as deep. It is to be aware of through observation, inquiry, or information. And our definition of "intimacy" is "closeness, friendship, and sexual intercourse". Our definition for "intimacy" is God's definition "to know Me".

His desire is to draw us into an intimate place where we explicitly trust Him allowing our hearts to be fully exposed. It's a way for us to connect deeply to Him through a relationship unlike anything we've ever experienced here on earth. God's intimacy is designed to unveil the deepest places of His love. There we will learn understand His character, experience His protection, and come to know a trust immeasurable by human standards. The intimate relationship with God will fortify our identity and develop within us a supernatural confidence of who we are in Him. Remember that whatever God has given us, the counterfeit is not far off. The The enemy's counterfeit intimacy lures us in because we are looking to fill what we are designed for -- intimacy. So we gravitate to the things that appear to fill these deep voids in our heart. Yet unlike the authentic, the counterfeit aims to change our name to something shameful. It destroys our confidence, robs us of our identity, steals our security, and condemns us through humiliation. The counterfeit eventually isolates us from the very thing we were after—love.

The enemy of this world has taken intimacy and perverted it and cheapened it to a sex act. Sex is sold, and used violently and abusively. In the world, intimacy has lost its beauty. So when the Lord welcomes us to experience Him intimately we stand there confused, or run in fear. God's design for intimacy is to make us complete in Him. It is our gift on earth to experience what eternity will be like with Him. However, the enemy has taken our bodies and hearts captive in his counterfeit stronghold

My heart rested behind an emotional wall of what I imagined would have been 42-inch thick bricks and a few hundred miles of barbed wire. Yet God was patient with me. He drew me out beyond the wall and began to restore to me the freedom that was stolen. If we move beyond the walls around our heart, the presence of the Lord will begin to restore what the enemy has stolen.

Friend, maybe you've never been sexually abused, but were betrayed by someone you trusted and now your heart resides behind a wall. The Holy Spirit desires to begin removing those stones, and give you the freedom your heart is longing for. "I will give you a new heart and put a new spirit in you; I will remove from you your heart of stone and give you a heart of flesh" (Ez. 36:26 NIV).

The Name of God

God wants to take the stones of your heart my friend, and build an altar with the very thing the enemy was using to destroy you. There He will meet you, and reveal Himself in ways you've never known before. God interacted and revealed His character to both Abraham and Moses at altars. Abraham made an altar and called it *Yahweh-Yireh*, the "Lord my provider" (see Ex. 22:29). Moses built an altar and called it *Yahweh-Nissi*, "the Lord is my standard" (see Ex. 17:15). David was known as a man after God's heart. To know God was his pursuit. When David built an altar for the Lord, he professed he would not bring to God an offering that didn't cost him something. He declared, "I love You, O Lord, my strength. The Lord is my rock and my fortress and my deliverer, My God, my rock, in whom I take refuge; My shield and the horn of my salvation, my stronghold" (Ps. 18:1–2).

David knew the many facets of God's character and attributes. Where Abraham and Moses only came to know a portion of God's character, David held the heart of God.

I was determined to learn to know the heart of God like King David. I wanted to be known as a woman after the heart of God. When I was crying out for deliverance, I had no idea the places God was going to touch and the wounds He was going to heal. Nevertheless, my suffering brought me to the throne of God, just as suffering had also brought Abraham, Moses, and David. Our weaknesses bring us to a place of desperation where we seek God no matter the cost. Such a pursuit unveils the character of God, and the intimate relationship He longs to have with us. My friend, God wants to reveal to you His many names so that you will come to know His character and He can re-establish trust between the two of you.

Journal Your Journey

Is your heart walled in?

- Draw an altar on the pages of your notebook.

- Write above the altar what or who hurt you.

- Record a prayer asking God to reveal His character at this altar.

I will give them a heart to know Me, for I am the LORD; and they will be My people, and I will be their God, for they will return to Me with their whole heart. (Jer. 24:7 NASB)

A Heart to Know Him

Testimony of Truth
Jaime's Story:

Growing up in a scientific home where the theory of evolution, the Big Bang, and survival of the fittest was her religion, Jaime learned to rationalize everything. Christianity was nothing more than mythical stories and the butt of jokes. God was hardly something worth considering.

Young and impressionable, Jaime learned her biological father had abandoned her before she was born. Life was difficult. She endured neglect, alcoholism, and for seven years she was sexually abused. At twelve years old, she confessed about the abuse, and was shamed into secrecy by a mother who didn't believe her.

Jaime felt discarded and ostracized. She responded by controlling every aspect of her life that she could. She worked hard not to need others. She found success in school, college, and life. In her mind, she was safest as the ruler of her life. While Jaime was preparing her own path, God was preparing a way to join her in the journey, and give her a heart to know Him.

Against impossible odds, she encountered her biological father. He shared with her stories of private investigators, as well as missing infor-mation about her and her mother's identity. She learned that after her father had exhausted all possible leads, he stopped looking and released it to God. For the first time Jaime encountered the reality of God.

Eventually, Jaime accepted the message of sal-vation, but when it came to the word of God and believing it was for her, she just couldn't get past the lies that were directly connected to her father's abandonment and the sexual abuse. She knew God as her Savior, but she didn't know the God of scriptures. She would read the Word, but there were roadblocks of rejection, inadequacy, and suspicion of scripture that would steal away the budding seeds placed in her heart.

One day Jaime came across the verse, "If you do not forgive others their trespasses [their reckless and willful sins, leaving them, letting them go, and giving up resentment], neither will your Father forgive you your trespasses" (Matt. 6:15).

Without warning, God touched a deep wound inside of her. The God of the scriptures was speaking directly to her. She knew He was asking her to forgive her abuser.

Jaime wrestled with doing something that would set her offender free and excuse away his offense.

God quickly spoke to Jaime's heart, assuring her He had something better for her beyond the pain.

Unwilling to ignore this personal encounter with God, she surrendered her heart to the thought of forgiving the perpetrator that had stolen her childhood. Then, one day she received a one-page typed letter signed by her abuser. The sentences combined admittance and recognition of the pain and suffering he caused her, and it was sealed with an apology.

At that very moment, on a white piece of paper, Jaime encountered Jehovah Rapha—the Lord who heals. She had come to know God through her suffering.

God gave Jaime a heart to know Him, and in her willingness to seek Him, He revealed Himself to her. God leaves nothing to chance. He is in constant pursuit of us with a desire that every heart He encounters would come to know Him. What a comfort we can take knowing that God not only pursues us, but also gives us the heart necessary to know Him. He wants to be our God, not from a distance but up close and personal. He wants to share His presence with us, and allow us to know every aspect of Him. Within the pages of scripture God is described as seeking, searching and pursuing. He is on a mission to encounter His people. His heart is to make Himself known to us, so that in return we would allow ourselves to be known by Him.

He has designed our hearts to be the center of our soul. Scripture says that out of our heart flows the direction of our lives. He longs to transform our hearts so that our direction in life will always be toward Him, and through our transformation others will come to know Him.

Over and over the Bible shares stories of God going after just the one in order to reach the multitude. In John 4:1–42, Jesus encounters a woman whose heart had been walled up. She is known as the woman at the well. Rejected because of her reputation and excluded because of her past, she lived in isolation from the people in the village. People discarded her, but God saw her. Jesus went out of His way to encounter this woman who had been rejected by so many. He addressed her sin and shame, but not in a way that made her shrink back into isolation. He accepted her right where she was, and He challenged the broken woman to be the woman He saw her to be—a woman healed and restored.

Her heart longed to know more of Him, and the more He shared, the hungrier she became for what He had. Meeting Christ allowed her to behold His presence. She accepted His freedom, and could not remain silent. Boldly she broke free from the shame, returned to the village that had rejected her. Confidently she shared what He had done. Her old life was gone, and there was nothing to be ashamed of anymore. Her transformation intrigued those who needed a Savior. Her freedom opened the door for others in the village to encounter Christ, and they too were liberated.

Friend, today Jesus is going out of His way to encounter you, just like He encountered Jaime, the woman at the well, and me. He wants to address your pain, not bring you shame. Your freedom and purpose are waiting beyond this wall. He intends to take the wounds that have buried you in the stronghold of the enemy, and set you free for His name's sake. He wants His name to be made known through you. He's chosen you and your story to reveal His character and attributes by sharing with other's the name God has revealed to you. When we learn who God is, how His character responds to our circumstances, and what He is known for, it rebuilds your trust for Him that was broken by others. When people see that you trust Him, they will be given a heart to know Him more. They will seek after the One you're talking about, and they will find Him.

Journal Your Journey

Here is your woman at the well moment. Jesus has come to give you freedom and purpose through it.

- Ask the Lord what He wants to do with your pain.

- Ask Him how you should respond to the pain.

- Ask Him how He will use it for His glory.

- Journal all He reveals to you.

The Secret Place

There is a secret place available to every believer, and the world does not know about it. The Lord calls this secret place His chambers. It's a place beyond the busy courtyard; this is a holy and sacred place. In the Old Testament it is where the priests would make their offerings to God. "The north and south rooms facing the temple courtyard are the priests' rooms . . . There they will put the most holy offerings—the grain offerings, the sin offerings, and the guilt offerings—for the place is holy (Ez. 42:13 NIV).

These are the most holy and sacred offerings:

The Grain Offering: Known as the most precious of offerings to the Lord. It is a voluntary act of worship, recognizing God's goodness and provision by a display of our devotion to Him.

The Sin Offering: An offering of our sin placed upon the altar, where He exchanges it with forgiveness and cleansing.

The Guilt Offering: Where the legal and emotional guilt from breaking the law or moral code are placed upon the altar so that restitution can be made.

Through Jesus Christ, we are now the royal priests who enter the chambers. You have been invited to approach the King. He is calling for your most holy offerings simultaneously—your sin and your worship. God knows that they have come at a great cost to you. But because of Jesus Christ, the debt for all of these offerings has been paid once and for all. We now stand in these chambers without fault.

> Yet now he has reconciled you to himself through the death of Christ in his physical body. As a result, he has brought you into his own presence, and you are holy and blameless as you stand before god without a single fault. (Col. 1:22)

Pause on that scripture and embrace the revelation. We stand before God faultless. So why do we keep holding on to the faults He no longer sees? Sometimes we need to physically walk it out, and lay down what we've been carrying around, in order to empty our hands and fully receive what He has for us. Today, the Lord is calling you to offer up to Him what no longer belongs to you. Let Him take you into the holy place and show you how righteously you stand before Him. Things that the world says are dishonorable and disgraceful, the King declares these are His most holy offerings. Our wounds, our shame, our struggles are sacred ground to Him and become precious offerings to place upon the altar before our King. Like David, we bring into the secret place an offering that has cost us something.

Journal Your Journey

You have been invited to enter into the chambers.

- Visualize what that looks like.

- Mentally approach His throne.

- Imagine laying the offerings upon the altar.

- Confess out loud what you are offering there.

- Declare you no longer own them.

- Record the experience in your journal.

When I enter into my time with the Lord it often looks like the meditative prayer we discussed in Chapter Five. I will lie on my back, secluded from others. I put on worship music and focus all of my attention on the image of the chambers, His face, and calming my breathing. If I find I'm mentally drifting off, I redirect myself. You might hear others call this "soaking." At first I found it challenging to settle my mind, so I would start with a small goal of 5 minutes. Now it's easy for me to take myself into a state of mind where I can enter into His chambers for an hour, drifting in and out of a rest in His presence like I've never experienced before.

Seek His Face

The King's chambers are filled with revelation and wonder. There is indescribable peace, and a closeness I have never known before. My only desire when I come into His chambers is to know the depth of His love for me. David wrote, "You have said, 'Seek my face.' My heart says to you, 'Your face, Lord, do I seek,'" (Ps 27:8 ESV) When I am in His presence that is my heart's cry.

How do we seek the face of the Lord? To answer that we must understand what the scripture says.

Biblical Hebrew for "face" is *paneh*: "appearance, presence, in the presence of, favor."

David is not speaking of a literal face. What David is writing about is a tangible presence, where seeking the face of God is to pursue an incredible appearance by the Creator of the world. God desires so much more for us than just making sure we live a happy life. He wants us to be in intimate relationship with Him, encountering one another on a level so vastly different than we ever could reach with people.

So many of us only know God through a petitioning-type relationship. We have never moved beyond seeking the hand of God. Our time spent with God has never gone beyond asking Him to move on our behalf. As His children this is our inheritance and our right; however, we have access to so much more. If we've never moved beyond the hand of God, we've missed out on an intimate presence. It's a place so close that it feels as though He has become one with you. My heart is that you will diligently search after and request the Lord to bring you to this place.

Do not believe the lie that your failures, or the wrongs done to you in the past, disqualify you to enter into the chamber of the King. He calls you to intimacy from right where you are. He desires that you know Him, so He will encounter you just as He encountered the woman at the well. He says, "Be still and know that I am God" (Ps. 46:10). The Hebrew word for "be still" is *raphah*, which literally means "to fail". Our failures are what we bring with us into the holy chambers of the King. We place these offerings upon the altar, and gaze upon the face of God. Our failures allow God the opportunity to shine His unfailing power, love, and presence through our brokenness. When He takes the mess and turns it into a message, then the world will see and know He is God.

My friend, the authentic and permanent stronghold of the Lord is His touchable, redemptive, and heart-pounding presence. It's the place where the invisible God becomes visible by connecting spirit to spirit. You, my sister, are safe and untouchable when you enter into this place. Can you now see why the enemy has attempted to destroy your trust through betrayal? He wants to keep you out of the very place you were meant to go when you've failed—the chambers of the King, where He awaits your offerings.

When God asked for my hidden secret it was to reveal a deeper portion of His love to me, and when He asked for Jaime to forgive, it was to take her somewhere better. We became like the woman at the well, bold and fierce about our freedom, and now we share it so others will know that God can be trusted. "For you are God, O Sovereign Lord. Your words are truth, and you have promised these good things to your servant" (2 Sam. 7:28).

> *Oh Father, how we rejoice in knowing that our past, our sins, our pain do not disqualify us from entering into your presence. How comforting it is to know that our shame is a sacred and holy offering to you. Here we kneel before your altar and lay down this ugly pain as a sacred and precious offering to you. Now, replace our hearts of stone, teach us to seek your face, and help us to know you deeper every day. Oh Most High King, take us deep into the Holy of Holies.*
>
> *We pray this in Jesus' name, amen.*

CHAPTER 7

We Have Overcome

*They overcame him by the blood of the lamb and the word of
their testimony; they did not love their lives so
much as to shrink from death.*

Rev. 12:11 (NIV)

*"When you can look a thing dead in the eye, acknowledge that
it exists, call it exactly what it is, and decide what role it will
take in your life then, my Beloved, you have taken the first step
toward your freedom." —Iyanla Vanzant*

I sat on the edge of my bed. "No, Lord! I can't teach
that!" I was stunned.

Early in the week I had been invited to teach a
breakout session at our women's retreat. On that day I
could barely contain myself. I was dancing around the
living room praising His name and rejoicing over the
opportunity to do what I love with the women of my
church. For the next week I prayed with anticipation
about a topic. When I got my answer, I wasn't so excited
anymore. Psalm 37:8 was the first verse He dropped into

my spirit. "Stop being angry! Turn from your rage! Do not lose your temper—it only leads to harm." The Lord was prompting me to teach on anger. Had He lost His mind?

At this time, my battle was known by less than a handful of women. I couldn't imagine sharing it with a classroom of women I hardly knew. I felt this was a cruel prank. I had longed to be a breakout speaker, and here was my first opportunity, but God wanted me to teach on the most shameful area of my life. Who was I to speak on anything that had to do with anger? I was the least qualified. My choices were obvious: decline the opportunity to do what I had dreamed to do, or obey God.

The journey to arrive at these words on the pages of this book started the day I said yes to God and no to my fear. I dove into scripture to find my answers and surprisingly uncovered my freedom. However, my freedom didn't come in my well-prepared message. It began with one act of obedience in the classroom at that retreat.

Armed that day with a solid biblical message on anger, I was walking into the small room when the Holy Spirit said, *tell them your story*. I pretended not to hear while I waited for the women to arrive. Again my spirit sensed, *tell them your story*. Nervously fidgeting, I played the "Is that God, or is that me?" card in order to buy myself a little extra time while I contemplated a way out. I may have even prayed for the sudden onset of a stomach virus. The women began filing in, and I overheard a few talking about the embarrassment they felt signing their name on the paper for class, as it had been labeled the "Anger Class." Again I heard, *tell them your story.* Now standing at the head of that class smiling on the outside, and wanting to run on the inside, a decision had to be made. Share the well-thought-out teaching on anger, or obey the Holy Spirit and tell my story. Twenty-five awkwardly smiling faces were awaiting a decision they didn't even know I had to make—and so began my journey.

My shame was attempting to dam up my words, as I opened with the confession of my most humiliating secret, *I have been diagnosed with Premenstrual Dysphoric Disorder . . .* and with every word that left my mouth I could feel a transformation happening. Unannounced to the women staring at me, I was being liberated. God was driving a stake in the ground, and He had the plumb line in His hand. He was declaring over my life Zechariah 4:10: "Do not despise these small beginnings, for the Lord rejoices to see the work begin, to see the plumb line in Zerubbabel's hand." I was being remade right before the eyes of these women. God was taking the stronghold of shame out of the hands of the enemy and setting me free by the power of my testimony. For whatever is kept in darkness the enemy has manipulating power over, but what is brought into the light he becomes powerless to. God was drawing me out of darkness and into the light of His glory. The broken vessel that stood before that classroom was experiencing a cleansing by His flowing, healing, living, and redeeming waters.

In that tiny room those gals and I laughed, cried, and connected on a level I don't think any of us were expecting. We prayed for one another, and I believe we all left feeling like a sisterhood had been formed. As I made my descent down the hill, it didn't take long for the enemy to attempt to drag me back into my fortress of shame. Thoughts were flooding my mind with the questions, *Did I over share? Would they gossip about me? Did I really hear from God?* However, when the Lord sets a daughter free, He doesn't leave her out in the open alone. He stands as her rear guard. God brought me a suddenly moment. I heard someone hollering my name from a distance. It was a lady from the breakout class. As I met her halfway, she started the conversation with these words, *Thank you for sharing; God connected with me in that classroom, and broke something off of me that I had been struggling with for a long time.* In that moment, God made it clear to me, my story is always safest in His hands.

The Word of Our Testimony

The two most powerful weapons we have as believers are the healing blood of Jesus Christ and our testimony of that healing. For so many of us, even though we've been set free and healed by His blood, shame has silenced our voices. We walk around cleansed and whole, but silenced by shame.

In the Old Testament, God had Israel make a chest and place it behind a veil in the Tent of Meeting. The chest was known as the Ark of the Testimony and it resided in a place called the Holy of Holies (see Ex. 30:6). Above the Ark were two cherubim, known as the Mercy Seat, and upon that seat the literal presence of God stayed. The Ark was veiled with a large curtain, and no one was allowed to go into the Holy of Holies except for Moses. However, once a year a pure priest would be allowed to enter the Holy of Holies to sprinkle blood on it for the restitution of Israel's sins. When Jesus died on the cross, scripture tells us that His death literally tore apart the veil that separated the Holy of Holies where the Ark of the Testimony was kept and the presence of God rested (see Matt. 27:50–51).

Today, because of what Jesus did on the cross, the Word says that you are now the temple, and the Spirit of the Lord resides in you (see 1 Cor. 3:16). Today, you are the living Ark of the Testimony, and because of God's mercy He now rests upon you. Each time you share your testimony, you break down the veil that separates others from God, and you welcome them into the Holy of Holies. Your testimony literally releases the purest form of God's presence that there is. Do you now see why your most powerful weapons are the blood of the Lamb and the word of your testimony? Together they are redemptive and restoring power. They are designed to set the captives free.

In the Old Testament, the Ark of the Testimony was a witness to the world that the Most High God was with Israel. Whether going into battle or traveling through new territory, the Ark went before them, and their enemies feared them. Today, you are that witness. Your testimony makes visible to the world an invisible God. We are the witnesses to our enemies that God is with us.

The enemy is aware of the power you and I possess, and his mission is to silence us. He wants the Holy of Holies veiled. If he can keep us thinking that God only shows up for an elite group of people, then people will underestimate their power and purpose on earth. My friend, we who hold the presence of God are not an elite group, we are an elect group. We've been set apart from this world, not from one another. Our jobs are to share our stories with our brothers and sisters in Christ, which will give them permission to share their stories. When we testify, we give witness to the fact that God is active among us. This in turn builds us up in the faith, releasing the presence of God amongst the Church, so we have the faith and hope to endure until His return.

Do not buy the lie that your story doesn't matter. Do not think that you have nothing to share. God has connected each one of us with a purpose and a plan, to make sure all of us end up in eternity with Him. Do not allow the enemy to take your voice away with feelings of insignificance or insecurities. You have been set free for a purpose. But don't be unwise; the enemy is not the only one who can veil the Ark of the Testimony within you. You hold the power to cover the Holy of Holies, too.

Unveiled Face

Every time we care more about the opinion of people than the opinion of God, and mask who we are in order to be accepted by others, we have personally veiled the Ark of the Testimony. God has not called us to live hidden behind a curtain of comparison, always worrying about the opinions of others. He has called us to live seen, as transformed women who know His opinion of us.

> But we all, with unveiled face, beholding as in a mirror the glory of the Lord, are being transformed into the same image from glory to glory, as from the Lord, the Spirit. (2 Cor. 3:18 NASB)

The word "glory" in the Greek is *dóksa*, and it means "to evoke a good opinion", i.e. that something has inherent, deep-down worth. A synonym for the word "mirror" is "reflect". Let's rewrite the scripture with this understanding: "But we, not wearing a mask, now *reflect the good opinion and inherent worth of the Lord*, are being *changed* into the same image from *good opinion* to *good opinion* from the Lord, the Spirit."

When we accept that there is only one opinion we should be concerned with, we move away from giving the opinion of others so much real estate. The more the Lord's view consumes our minds, the more we are transformed, right up to the point where our lives actually reflect what He says we are. What exactly does God say of you?

133

> He *made peace with everything* in heaven and on earth by means of Christ's blood on the cross. This includes you who were once far away from God. You were his enemies, separated from him by your evil thoughts and actions. Yet now he has reconciled you to himself through the death of Christ in his physical body. As a result, he has brought you into his own presence, and you are *holy* and *blameless* as you stand before him *without a single fault.* (Col. 1:20–22, emphasis mine)

My friend, you have nothing to be ashamed of, and not a single reason to wear a mask. God is at peace with who you are. His opinion of you is that you are holy, blameless, and without one fault. When you accept that opinion about yourself, it will transform you from the inside out, and you will no longer be silenced in shame, but you will boldly share your testimony with others. It's a magnificent revelation to know His opinion.

Testimony of Truth
Lisa's Story:

> *My healing began when I was tired of running and tired of the lies I had told to protect my eating disorders and addictions. I didn't just need to heal physically from all the damage I had done to my body from 22 years of disordered eating and prescription medications. I had to heal the deepest part of my soul that I had been numbing most of my life. In my addictions, I hurt the ones*

I loved the most, and my marriage and relation-ships with my family needed to be restored.

The beginning of my recovery was very difficult. I really did not know how to be free from bondage. I did not know who I was without them. I did not know anything different than to suffer, so I really had to go out on a limb and trust the process, and to trust Jesus through the process.

I had tried and failed recovery more times than I care to admit. I did know one thing; I was tired of doing life on my terms, and trusting in drugs or my eating disorder to get me through rather than Jesus. I was completely ready to do anything, and if that meant to trust and lean on Jesus to heal me then that was what I would do.

I knew getting connected to church was what I needed, even though I had my reservations about doing so, but I did it anyway. I literally took one day at a time, and for the first six months I felt like I was going to suffocate with the bombard-ment of feelings I did not know how to handle, or even recognize where they were coming from.

My healing came, the more I was obedient to Je-sus and what he wanted for my life. The real test came when my pastor asked me to tell my story on Easter Sunday. I said yes because I knew this was what Jesus wanted me to do. Being obedient was the best thing I could have ever done for my healing.

Through my testimony, I watched my husband's walls come tumbling down, and I saw through the tears streaming down his face what forgiveness looked like. God was healing my husband through my story. After the service, God opened dialog with other women who were where I once used to be. Today I hear stories from others of how my testimony helped restore their lives.

In times of doubt, when I wanted to give up, I pressed into God all the more. I know the enemy is out to get me and he wants me back, but knowing what I know now, I will never go back. I will never forget where I was when I hit rock bottom, and how much despair I was in. Remembering where I was makes me thankful for where I am in my life.

Lisa believed the good opinion of the Lord and obeyed His direction. She did not cower under shame and insecurities, and she refused to wear the mask. When she doubted, she did not look to her own thinking, but pressed into Jesus for deeper understanding and revelation.

Waiting For Your Healing

I approached the Lord contending to be healed from Pre-menstrual Dysphoric Disorder, and He healed me from so much more. My narrow focus was a deliverance from a diagnosis but God's focus was a broad deliverance from the stronghold of shame. I may not yet be healed from PMDD, but I certainly overcame it. I allowed the Lord to come in and heal the parts of my life I didn't realize needed healing and now this disorder no longer manages my life, I manage it. I am off of anti-depressants, and my fits of anger are few and far between. I cannot remember the last episode of rage, so to me that's a victory.

> You intended to harm me, but God intended it for good to accomplish what is now being done, the saving of many lives. (Gen. 50:20 NIV)

He takes the very thing the enemy is attempting to destroy us with, and He uses it to save the lives of others through the power of our testimony. Sometimes our healing doesn't come in an instant and other times it does. Through my journey, God had a story to tell, and there is one being written about your journey too. My friend, do not think your testimony is invalid because you are not fully restored; your testimony gives witness to a God who is walking the road with you. So do not be discouraged by the results. The Lord is doing so much more than healing you—He's making Himself known in the process.

Not on Your Own

Our time together is coming to a close. Soon you and I will go our separate ways. So like any good friend, I want to leave you with some parting wisdom. By now you've established a regular routine of spending time with the Lord. You are regularly journaling, and pursuing consistent quiet time, and you've added to your secret place a few of the new things you've learned throughout this study. It's easy to slide out of this routine once the book has come to an end. So, I want to remind you of the trap to attempt to sustain where you are today on your own.

> How foolish can you be? After starting your Christian lives in the Spirit, why are you now trying to become perfect by your own human effort? (Gal. 3:3)

Everything we did through the pages of this book included the Power of the Holy Spirit, the redemption of Jesus Christ, and the authority of God. Be alert that you do not attempt to keep your freedom apart from it. We were never designed to live perfectly apart from them.

The English definition for "perfect" is: "free from any flaw or defect in condition or quality; faultless". I want to you wipe that definition out of your mind when it comes to anything you read about perfection in the New Testament.

The Greek word for "perfect" is *teleios* and the definition is "complete; mature". When we operate in partnership with Christ, we are brought to a level of perfection through Him. He is what makes us complete. He is the only one who lived up to the standard of perfection that we think about when we hear the word "perfect", and because He did, we don't have to. Now He desires for us to share in His perfection and be made complete within Him. "After you have suffered for a little while, the God of all grace who called you to His eternal glory in Christ, will himself perfect, confirm, strengthen, and establish you" (1 Pet. 5:10 NASB).

Friend, don't attempt to live at the standard of freedom He has shown you through this study apart from Him—it's certain disaster. To ensure you maintain this level of freedom I want you to purpose to live connected.

Live Connected

While we were created to abide in the authentic stronghold with God the Father, God the Son, and God the Holy Spirit, we were also designed for fellowship with one another.

> Do not give up meeting together, as some are in the habit of doing, but encourage one another—and all the more as you see the Day approaching. (Heb. 10:25 NIV)

God commanded us to remain connected. We need each other to make it to the end. Your stories, gifts, and wisdom, coupled with the stories, gifts, and wisdom of another is what makes the body of Christ and causes it to function and accomplish all that God has for it to accomplish. My story, Lisa's story, and the power of God's spirit are for the purpose of building one another up. "So encourage each other and build each other up, just as you are already doing" (1 Thess. 5:11).

I would challenge you. Take your book, and start your own group. You've gone down the journey and you are able to take someone else down the path too. It's important that we live our life following someone who is farther ahead of us, and leading someone who is just behind us. There is too much work to do for us to leave it for another. You don't have to know it all, but just share what you know to someone who doesn't know it. Do not agree with the lie that your knowledge is insufficient, because what God has called you to, He will equip you for. Now go find her and lead her.

Journal Your Journey

- Pray that God would connect you to the one ahead of you.

- Now pray to be connected to the one behind you.

- Ask the Lord what He wants you to do with your story.

- Journal what you sense the Spirit is saying

Live in Unity

As women we can be hardest on our own kind. We judge, ignore, hold grudges, and gossip about each other. If the enemy can keep us focused on an offense or our sister's shortcomings, he will make our sister our enemy, and we will be fighting on the wrong front. Friend, it's time we begin being part of the solution instead of aiding the enemy in his fight to divide.

> For we are not fighting against flesh-and-blood enemies, but against evil rulers and authorities of the unseen world, against mighty powers in this dark world, and against evil spirits in the heavenly places. (Eph. 6:12)

I will never forget a vision God gave me one day while my children were arguing. As they stood face to face bickering about who knows what, I saw that standing beside both of them was the Father of Lies. Although the kids thought they were fighting each other, they were actually fighting him. He was whispering words of doubt, jealously, suspicion, and envy within their ears. They ripped each other apart with their words while the Father of Lies stood back and wickedly smirked.

Unless we recognize whom we are fighting, we will fall for that each and every time. We are our sister's keeper. In battle we face our enemies, and we stand arm and arm with our comrades. Whom are you facing in battle and whom are you standing alongside? If it's a sister you are facing, then you're fighting the wrong enemy, and you've joined the fight with a liar. Remember, we are stronger together than we will ever be apart. We were never designed to run the race alone; we were designed to run it in unity. "He makes the whole body fit together perfectly. As each part does its own special work, it helps the other parts grow, so that the whole body is healthy and growing and full of love" (Eph. 4:16).

Our love for one another and the stories of our lives will bring revelation to a dying world that there is a safe stronghold for them to take refuge in. "Your love for one another will prove to the world that you are my disciples" (John 13:35).

My dear friend, be brave, be bold, be tender, be forgiving, be kind, be generous, be accepting, and be faithful to one another. Obey the leading of the Holy Spirit and share your story for the benefit of another. Remember, your testimony is the witness to the faithfulness of a living God, and it says, "What God did for me, He will do for you, too."

Oh, what a journey this has been. The Lord has taken the very thing the enemy attempted to destroy me with, and He's used it to make His Name known in the earth. Now you have a journal full of your own journey—Go and do likewise.

Lord, Jesus, you have been so merciful to us as we've trekked out of captivity and into your stronghold. Keep us wise to the lies and keep our ears tuned to your voice. Father, we know this is only the beginning, and we declare that by the power of the Holy Spirit we will take our lives, redeemed through Jesus Christ, and use them to make you known within our sphere of influence. Give us the boldness, courage and grace to live a life pleasing to you.

In your mighty name we pray, amen.

Stronghold — The secrets beyond the wall

144

End Notes

Chapter 1: The Stronghold

1. Renee Swope, *A Confident Heart*, (Grand Rapids, MI, Baker Publishing, 2011)

Chapter 2: A Friend For the Journey

1. Charles Haddon Spurgeon, *The Metropolitan Tabernacle Pulpit: Sermons Preached and Revised, Volume 24* (London : Passmore & Alabaster, 1883-1916.)

2. Roland Herbert Bainton, *Here I Stand*, (Peabody, MA: Hendrickson Publishers, 2009)

Chapter 4: Take Captive Those Thoughts

1. Dr. Caroline Leaf, *Switch Your Brain On*, (Grand Rapids, MI: Baker Publishing Group, 2013)

Chapter 5: Bondage Of Busyness

1. Lysa TerKeurst, *The Best Yes*, (Nashville, TN: Nelson Books, 2014)

2. Jeff Goins, *What Does It Mean To Minister To The Lord*, www.jeffgoins.myadventures.org

Chapter 6: Trust His Name

1. National Institute of Justice & Centers for Disease Control & Prevention, *Prevalence, Incidence, and Consequences of Violence Against Women Survey,* 1998.

2. U.S. Department of Justice, *2003 National Crime Victimization Survey,* 2003.

   U.S. Bureau of Justice Statistics, *Sex Offenses, and Offenders 1997,* 1998.

   Commonwealth Fund, *Survey of the Health of Adolescent Girls,* 1998.

   World Health Organization, 2002.

3. Carol J. Cook, Ph.D and Cindy L. Guertin, MAMFT, *"How Childhood Sexual Abuse Affects Adult Survivors' Images of God"* http://www.aapc.org/media/47481/cookguertin.pdf

19546356R00090

Made in the USA
San Bernardino, CA
04 March 2015